CAMBERLEY & YORKTOWN
BETWEEN THE WARS

GRAHAM BARSON

SUTTON PUBLISHING

Sutton Publishing Limited
Phoenix Mill · Thrupp · Stroud
Gloucestershire · GL5 2BU

First published 2007

Copyright © Graham Barson, 2007

Title page photograph: Camberley Carnival.
'The Costers' Day Out', posing in Upper
Charles Street.

British Library Cataloguing in Publication Data
A catalogue record for this book is available from the
British Library.

ISBN 978-0-7509-4540-0

Typeset in 10.5/13.5 Photina.
Typesetting and origination by
Sutton Publishing Limited.
Printed and bound in England by
J.H. Haynes & Co. Ltd, Sparkford.

CONTENTS

STREET PLAN OF

FRIMLEY
AND
CAMBERLEY

Scale

0   1/4   1/2 MILE
0   1000   2000   2640 FEI

Urban District Boundary — · — · —

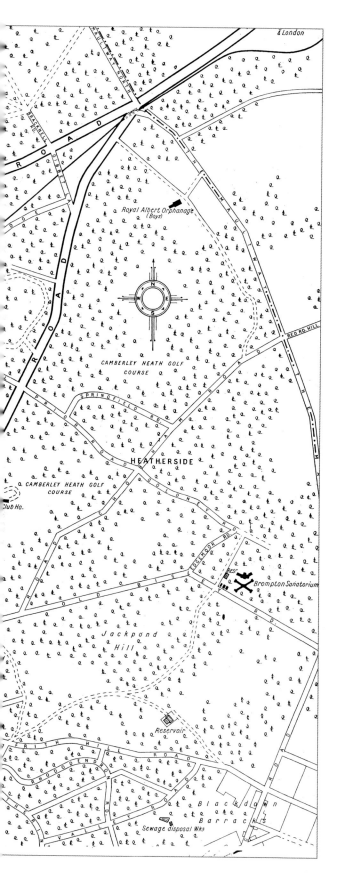

Street plan of Frimley and Camberley, *c.* 1934.

St Michael's Church, Camberley.

ACKNOWLEDGEMENTS

This book was compiled in conjunction with Surrey Heath Museum, to whom I am indebted, and I wish to thank them for their time and the use of their local archives and other facilities. In particular, I would like to thank Mary Bennett, Assistant Curator, not only for her energy and enthusiasm for the book but also for her considerable contribution to the informative captions; her detailed knowledge of the Camberley area is quite extraordinary. Special thanks also go to Graham Dennis, who located the album of photographs, duly remembered my interests in the Camberley area and suggested it would make a great book – well here it is. I would also like to thank the following individuals for their assistance with the book: Mrs Alexander, my wife Sandy Barson, Les Burberry, John End, Mr A. Gibbons, Dusty Miller, Ted Smith, and R.M. Woodruff.

While every effort has been made to establish copyright and permission sought to reproduce material where appropriate, the author and publisher apologise for any omissions and will be happy to rectify these in any future edition.

A view that would have been familiar to generations of people living in the Camberley area as another military camp set up its tents on the common. From the time of James I there had been summer camps on the Bagshot heathland and, even though the Royal Military College and Staff College were built to house and train Officer Cadets and Senior Staff, there was still the problem of temporary accommodation for the rank and file. As late as the Second World War a similar camp was erected on Barossa Common where some of the men returning from Dunkirk in 1940 were housed. The tents were gradually replaced with Nissen huts used for the Free French troops and then German prisoners of war. When housing was erected in the area known as the Old Dean Estate, Lorraine School was named in memory of this French connection.

Open heathland near Heatherside Corner in Camberley, photographed in the 1930s, looking much as it had done for centuries, with a network of paths crossing through low-growing heather and gorse. The whole of the area, now known as Camberley, would have looked like this before the Enclosure Act of 1801, when the bulk of the land was allotted to local landowners and fenced off according to the size of the allotment. Vast acres of land were planted with fir trees and other plots were used as small estates, with a large house surrounded by a woodland garden. Traditionally, many people would have travelled through the area over a myriad of small tracks, similar to those seen here, and would only have used the Turnpike Road or the London Road from Bagshot to Blackwater if they were travelling in a coach or with a laden wagon.

INTRODUCTION

Historically, the Camberley area was part of the open heathland surrounding the small village of Frimley, with its Manor House at Frimley Park. There were no traditional industries in the area other than small-scale farming in the Blackwater Valley. In 1801 this land was enclosed and thousands of acres were planted with fir trees. For centuries the heathland north of the Surrey Heath villages had been used for military manoeuvres and, with the building of the Royal Military College at Sandhurst in 1812, the area, now known as Yorktown, was developed to house those required to serve this new industry.

A one-sided high street which extended to Camberley (after the building of the Staff College in 1862) was lined with shops and trades associated with providing for this military presence. On the outskirts of the town, large heavily wooded private estates were built and the area was marketed as a 'health resort': 'Amid the Pine Woods of the Surrey Hills – the Arcachon of England'. Many of the residents were ex-military personnel who retired in Camberley, having trained in the town as young men, and in the 1930s the town acquired the name of 'Colonelstown'. Many of the tradesmen had army training and they set up primarily as service industries to the Army, including military tailors and bootmakers, and a number of laundries. The mid-war period saw a growth of ribbon development along the Frimley Road and the development of Tekels Park and the Watchetts Estate, where large houses surrounded by parkland had been sold off in small plots. The first small-scale industries moved to Camberley just before the Second World War, with several being established here to avoid the bombing in London.

The inspiration for this book was the discovery and purchase of an archive of photographs taken of the Camberley area between 1920 and 1940, the majority of which are previously unpublished. It appears likely that the photographs were taken by W. Marshall & Son, photographers of 25 London Road, Camberley, or Charles E. Smith, who worked for Marshall. The Marshalls did not live or trade in Camberley, as far as can be determined, until after the First World War. In 1923 William Edward and his wife Emma Marshall were living above the shop. By the early 1930s they were living at Langley in Woodlands Road and their son, William Donald Cecil Marshall, was living at Iona, also in Woodlands Road, with his wife Constance Maud. It is possible that Mr Marshall was an army photographer as he did not appear to advertise his business, although one strange advert did appear in the *Camberley News* over a five-week period in 1921:

6 May 1921:   This space is taken by Marshalls
13 May 1921:   Who is Marshall?
10 June 1921: To the Amateur Photographer
                        Courteous Reception
                        Instruction in the use of Cameras
                        Developing, Printing, Enlarging
                        Marshall's and Son, 25 London Road, Camberley

W.E. Marshall's output of photographs of the Military and Staff College was considerable, but he may have produced only limited numbers of photographs of Camberley and the surrounding area; with some appearing in the *Camberley News*.

William Edward Marshall died in November 1935 and is buried in St Michael's churchyard. His wife Emma was buried with him in 1941. There were no obituaries in the local press for either William Edward or Emma. William Jnr went into partnership with Mr Vaughan, who had been a press photographer, and sold the business to Mr Vaughan in December 1959. It now seems likely that the archive of photographs used in this book was the property of Charles E. Smith of Aspen Cottage, Charles Street, Camberley, who was responsible for processing the films taken by Marshall and other customers of the shop. He was a pupil of Yorktown School and later became the Assistant Secretary and Treasurer of the Yorktown School Old Boys' Association. He led a very active life; he was a member of the St John Ambulance Brigade, Honorary Secretary of the Comrades of the Great War in 1920 and organised fund-raising events. He was also Honorary Secretary of the Frimley and Camberley Motor Ambulance Committee and the Camberley and District Rifle Club. He was also a special constable and, in addition, a photographer.

1

Royal Military &
Staff College, Camberley

The Royal Military College in Sandhurst is now known as the Royal Military Academy.
Designed by James Wyatt, it opened to the first batch of young cadets in 1812.
Although Turnpike Road crossed the southern boundary of the land, almost all the
building materials were carried on the Basingstoke Canal. They were then transported
by horse and cart from the wharf at Frimley Green. It took almost eleven years to
build and much of the first five years was spent in landscaping the grounds and in
making bricks, which were found to be substandard and were never used.

A view across the lake and landscaped gardens looking towards New College on a very cold day in the 1930s. The grounds were laid out by Mr Bracebridge, a follower of Capability Brown, soon after the land was purchased in 1801; the college buildings were completed in 1812. It is said that Napoleonic prisoners of war were used to dig out the lake, although there is no evidence to support this legend. The stream which passes through the college grounds was originally used to power a small mill and the mill-pond was subsequently enlarged over a number of years to form the two lakes that are situated between the buildings and the southern boundary of the estate. In the *Annals of Sandhurst* Major Mockler-Ferryman states that sand and gravel taken out of the lake was 'banked up to conceal the ground floor of the building'. He goes on to say that 'during the Peninsular War, when numbers of militia regiments were embodied, it was deemed advisable to keep the men employed, and three or four regiments were encamped on the common in the rear of the College to furnish working parties to improve the estate. From the accounts we learn that upwards of 3,000 loads of soil were removed in country carts at sixpence a load, the rest of the work being done by militia-men and their shovels.'

New College was built in the grounds of the Royal Military College in the early twentieth century. Designed by Mr H.B. Measures, who was the Director of Barrack Construction, it was built to house the growing number of cadets in adequate living accommodation. Work started in 1908 and the first cadets moved in during September 1911. A narrow tramway was constructed from Blackwater station to carry materials to the site, and the old gymnasium, which is now the library, was used as a temporary railway terminus.

A winter's view across the lake in front of the Royal Military College, with the boat-house, which was erected to house the rowing boats used by the cadets for training and pleasure. In this photograph the lake appears to be almost frozen over and a close watch would have been kept on it by local people as well as the cadets, who would enjoy skating on the ice almost every winter.

Queen Mary and one of her ladies in waiting leaving the rear of the Royal Military College building after attending the opening of the enlarged chapel in 1937. It was one of the many functions that the Royal Family have graced over the years, the annual Passing Out Parade being the most frequently attended. This exit leads from what is now the Indian Army Memorial Room, which was initially used as a chapel and later as the dining hall.

Opposite, top: The Royal Military College Chapel was erected in 1879. It was built on the same line as the original chapel, now the Indian Army Memorial Room, that is, from north to south, with the altar at the south end, rather than the usual east to west. In the early twentieth century the layout was changed and the building enlarged, a new chancel and sanctuary were built at the east end and the former sanctuary was retained as a chapel of remembrance. In 1921 the new building was re-consecrated by the Archbishop of Canterbury. The walls and columns within the chapel are lined with memorials to men who attended the college and went on to lose their lives in conflicts around the world.

Opposite, bottom: The Staff College was erected in 1862 on open heathland just north of an area known, in 1851, as Mud Town, which is now the town of Camberley. It was designed by James Pennethorne, a pupil of John Nash, and the foundation stone was laid in December 1859 by HRH the Duke of Cambridge. The settlement opposite this new building initially became known as Cambridge Town. The building originally had only the first three floors, with low towers at each end and a central pediment. The additional floor, faced with slate, was added just before the First World War.

Part of the display of china and paintings set up in the new Royal Military College Library and Museum, which opened in 1931. The cases contain a collection of pottery and china donated by Colonel Crookshank. There were some rare items, including a Lambeth delft-ware dish, *c.* 1690, depicting Charles II hiding in an oak tree. The walls were lined with oil paintings of military men and royalty. Portraits of George III and Queen Charlotte and their eldest son, later George IV, and his brother Frederick, Duke of York, after whom the local area of Yorktown was named, used to hang there.

Opposite: Two views of the interior of the Royal Military College Library, when it opened in 1931. Known as the Central Library, as it is situated between the Royal Military College and the Staff College, it houses an impressive collection of books on military history and the archive of both colleges. Held here are important artefacts, including the Duke of Wellington's Field Order Book and the pen used to sign the surrender of the Japanese Expeditionary Force to Lord Mountbatten in 1945.

A military funeral was always a wonderful spectacle in Camberley, where the procession would proceed out of the Staff College gates and along the London Road towards St Michael's Church. If the service was held at St George's they would pass through the town, or if at St Paul's they would carry on up Church Hill before making the return journey to St Michael's or carrying on to Frimley for burial. On most occasions, a gun carriage would be used to carry the coffin draped in the union flag and current and ex-military men would walk alongside the carriages. Here the carriage has stopped by one of the lodges at the entrance to the Staff College.

The Camberley War Memorial, which stands just outside the entrance to the Staff College in the London Road, was erected in memory of local men who lost their lives during the First World War. The War Office granted a 999-year lease on the land, and in 1921 trees that had stood on the site were felled to make way for the memorial, which was to be surrounded by a gravel path and lawns. A latin cross, hewn from grey Cornish granite, was unveiled by the Duke of Connaught on 30 August 1922. Local residents raised £2,000, and of this £700 was spent on purchasing the cross, its delivery from Penryn, laying out the base and the grounds and etching the names. The remaining money was used to endow beds at the Frimley Cottage Hospital. Before the erection of this memorial there was a war shrine at St George's Church, where wreaths were laid to commemorate Armistice Day.

2

London Road

During the 1920s and '30s the London to Exeter route was still the main road to the south-west. With the increase in road transport during this period tearooms sprang up along the route to cater for holidaymakers and other travellers. The Jolly Tea Rooms, shown in the photograph, were built in 1926 opposite the Jolly Farmer Inn for Mr Alfred Frederick Stevens, and opened in November of that year. In 1932 they were owned by Mr H.W. Bolton.

The London Road carried all traffic through the town of Camberley when travelling to the west country until the M3 opened in the early 1970s. The road was the busiest in the area. This was a one-sided High Street to the military colleges serving their needs by providing shops, public houses, churches and recreational facilities, with the two settlements of Yorktown and Camberley running off it. Before the building of the colleges it had been a turnpike road and the milestones can still be seen along its length from the 28-mile stone near the Jolly Farmer to the 30-mile stone nestling in the front wall of the old parade of shops in Yorktown. Between the two world wars it contained a number of road-side cafés, the first public toilets for many miles for passing travellers, and was still a busy shopping area for the local community.

The Jolly Farmer Inn is situated on a roundabout between the A325 Portsmouth Road and the A30, the old London to Exeter turnpike road, and is currently a golf retail outlet; it closed as a public house on 9 November 1996. The name Jolly Farmer (formerly the Golden Farmer) was first given to the building on the transfer of a licence on 19 June 1823, the name Golden being removed and Jolly inserted. It was suggested that the new name was given to the inn because of the cheerful expression of William Davis on the signboard. William Davis, who is said to have occupied the original building off Maultway North, was thought to be the notorious seventeenth-century Golden Farmer highwayman. He was born into a farming community in North Wales, and later moved to a farmhouse bordering Bagshot Heath. This heathland was traversed by the London to Exeter road, much used by wealthy merchants and livestock dealers who were targeted by the highwaymen who terrorised the area. By day William Davis successfully managed a farm in the Bagshot area for over forty years and was the pillar of society; but at night-time, he would rob the rich and poor of their jewellery, gold and money. He was nicknamed the Golden Farmer because he paid all his debts in gold. Using clever disguises, he somehow managed to elude the authorities for almost fifty years. The Golden Farmer was reportedly caught in Southwark in October 1690 and executed in December of the same year, his body was then hanged in chains on Bagshot Heath, which is why a road nearby is called Gibbett Lane. New evidence has recently revealed that there may be an error in the identity of the Golden Farmer, who may in fact have been named John Bennet. The original inn was later used as the Golden Farmer Post Office in 1853.

A very quiet afternoon on a sunny day in 1937 when the narrow London Road between the Jolly Farmer and Camberley could cope very well with the number of cars using it. At this time the pavement was almost as wide as the road and any pedestrians could happily stroll along this tree-lined route on a pleasant afternoon.

The local firm of Spear & King, who had their yard in Gordon Road, Camberley, was carrying out work to Tudor House when this photograph was taken. In 1934, major alterations took place to update this Victorian mansion and convert it into a hotel. The number of men employed on a project as extensive as this can be judged from their bicycles propped up in the front garden.

Tudor House, also known as the Tudor Hotel, was one of the first houses built in the new Cambridge Town. It was occupied in 1867 by Captain Sydney Farrell, who was probably attached to the Staff College, which opened in 1862. In 1889 Dr James Hamilton Scott and his wife Kate moved here and occupied it until the 1920s. In 1929 Mrs Ethel Thunder purchased the property and the house had a brief change of name when it became known as Thunderleigh. It was sold to Mrs Bertha Baird in 1934 and while owned by Mrs Baird it was converted into the Tudor Hotel. As it was situated next to the Blue Pool on the main route from London to the west country it was ideally suited for this purpose. Sadly, because of the outbreak of the Second World War it was used as a hotel for only a few years. The house was demolished when the Blue Pool closed. A new block of flats named Tudor Court has been erected in its place.

The Cambridge Hotel in the late 1920s. The building had originally been designed with Dutch-style elevations, which were removed in 1921 when the hotel accommodation was extended into the former attic rooms. Here the building is shown just before the addition of the barn and new entrance, which were erected in the area between the hotel and White's Garage, which can be seen on the left. The glass constructions on the roof of the building behind the hotel are the roof-lights in Woolworth's store, which had its entrance in the High Street.

Stacks of reclaimed timber lay in front of the partially erected extension to the Cambridge Hotel in the 1930s, when Spear & King, a local building company, rebuilt what had been an agricultural barn that adjoined the hotel. During this inter-war period many local barns and timber-framed buildings were removed from their original sites and re-erected. This addition to the hotel was initially used for dinners, dances and functions, including fashion displays. It is currently used as a night club.

The Cambridge Hotel in Camberley, on the corner of the London Road and the High Street, photographed in the 1930s when White's Garage used this prominent corner of the ground floor as a showroom. The hotel was built for Captain Charles Raleigh Knight who owned all the land on which Camberley stands and was responsible for laying out the grid pattern of streets, and for building many of the earliest buildings. Erected in 1862, it was built opposite the new Staff College to cater for visitors to this rapidly developing area of former heathland. It was named after the Duke of Cambridge, who was Commander-in-Chief of the Army at this time, and the new town was known as Cambridge Town.

Scaffolding erected at the front of new shops being built in the London Road, near Sparvell Way, February 1932. Initially there were two clubs for men next to one another: the West Surrey Club, which used to meet at the building just behind these shops, and the Camberley and District Club, which is the building on the right. The Camberley and District Club, which was established before 1907, was reconstructed and extended in 1934. It still stands next to Sparvell Way today.

The old pump at the rear of the former Aspen Tree public house, which stood on the corner of Lower Charles Street in the London Road, Camberley, in the 1930s. The pub closed as a licensed premises in December 1925 and, until the 1980s when it was demolished, it was used by various shopkeepers. In 1938 it was occupied by P. Read, a pastrycook and confectioner.

Staff House in the London Road, Camberley, just before it was demolished in 1936 to make way for the new post office. It was the home of local builder and Frimley & Camberley Urban District Councillor Harry Doman, who had lived in the house since the 1890s. The shop to the right was owned by A.J. Searle, a furniture dealer. Two houses on the left, known as Staff Villas, had been demolished in the early 1930s to make way for the Arcade Cinema.

The site of Staff House in the London Road cleared to enable the new post office to be built on the site in 1937. Built by Francis Bros of Tilehurst, the new neo-Georgian offices were officially opened by Mrs Dorothy Worsley on 9 September 1937. When opened, the interior was described as light and spacious with panelled oak walls, a public table for writing and four chairs for customers. The sorting office was at the rear of the building off Upper Charles Street.

One of the ornate gas lamps on the London Road, at the corner of Lower Charles Street, decorated with a garland of flowers to celebrate either the Silver Jubilee of George V in 1935 or the Coronation of George VI in 1937. The flags pinned across the trees are in front of St Tarcisius's Church, and beyond these further decorations can just be seen in front of the shops occupied by Conway Williams, a local tailor, and the Corner House Tea Rooms.

The front of the London Road Recreation Ground with the original railings and mature trees that lined the London Road, in the late 1920s. At the centre is the Abbot-Anderson fountain and two of the temporary wooden pavilions used by sportsmen and spectators when matches were held on this ground.

This water fountain was erected in memory of Major-General Edward Abbot-Anderson, who lived in Royden House in Heathcote Road. He died in December 1903 after living for most of his 71 years in the Camberley area, initially as a student cadet, then as an instructor and eventually as a professor. After his death a Memorial Committee was set up to raise money by public subscription as a mark of respect to a man who was well known for supporting the Local Volunteers, Rifle Club, Horticultural Association and the Primrose League. The original aim was to erect a drinking fountain with a cattle trough attached and a clock at the top of the structure, but because of the cost this more modest memorial was built. It was designed and made by a local firm of stonemasons owned by Mr Adkins. Major Abbot-Anderson's son, also named Edward, became a well-known actor under the stage name of Allan Aynsworth.

The storm of 10 and 11 July 1927 caused major flooding in the area. The London Road and many side roads were transformed into rushing rivers; the water was many inches deep and did not subside until the next morning. Several cars had their windows broken by the force of the huge hailstones, some of which were reported as being 1½in square. The greater part of Camberley High Street was also flooded, with water pouring into many of the shops. The torrential downpour left a river of water down the main London Road, just at the front of the recreation ground. The shops from the Recreation Ground end are A. Baker & Sons, picture framers; C.H. Hamer, the hairdressers and tobacconist; and Plater & Sons, baker and confectioner, with the 'Teas' sign above the door. The shops set slightly forward to the road were the original White's Garage premises, with Jones & Sons, decorators, nearest to the camera.

Built in the mid-nineteenth century, Pembroke Cottages on the London Road were situated between the Frimley & Camberley Urban District Council offices and the Avenue Inn. When this photograph was taken in 1931 Mrs Catchpole, Mr Allen and Mrs Daybourne lived in the cottages.

The Avenue Inn or beer house on the London Road, formerly known as The Eagle, photographed in the mid-1930s. Behind the inn is the tower of the fire station with some of the large houses in The Avenue beyond. This public house opened in 1851 as one of the many small drinking establishments catering for working-class men. The Sadler & Baker sign, advertising the sale of this land, is in the front garden of Pembroke Cottages. The land was purchased by the Woking Co-operative Society as the site for its new store, for which planning permission was granted in November 1933.

These buildings used to stand between the Avenue Inn and The Avenue, with the Central Hall and the Methodist church visible beyond the entrance to the road. The people standing outside the shop could be Mr and Mrs Albert James Harding, who ran the family business of decorators and carpenters from these premises, which had a workshop at the rear. Beyond this shop was a private house occupied by Miss Duck. Percy Walker Stoodley owned the next shop called Stoodley & Co., electricians, and the last house in this row is a tiny single-storey cottage which was occupied by Emma Joselyn. All that can be seen of this cottage is the wooden arch between the gate and the front door. These buildings were demolished in the 1980s.

The demolition of Osnaburgh House, Osnaburgh Parade, the London Road. It is thought that Osnaburgh House was built from materials surplus to requirements at Farnborough Hill, the home of Empress Eugenie, before 1870. It was occupied by a number of military men attached to the Royal Military College. Colonel Bethel Martin Dawes lived there in 1886 when there was an outbreak of diphtheria, caused by contaminated milk supplied by a Frimley dairy. His son George and his daughter Mary were only two of a number of children from the upper-class houses in the area who died from the disease. The children of Captain Brown, Captain O'Sullivan, Dr Scott and one of the daughters of Dr Muller of Crosby Hill, three-year old Elsa, were some of the victims, all of whom appeared to come from well-off families. The report in the *Lancet* concluded that poor families were not affected because milk was never stored in their homes. They would purchase a small amount each morning, which would normally be consumed at breakfast time, usually in their tea. The homes where servants were employed would store the milk so that it was available all day for the family and their visitors. They were also more likely to give milk as a drink to their children, and the milk would rarely have been boiled before they drank it. In all there were fifty-one cases of diphtheria, seventeen of which proved fatal. Another occupant of the house before its demolition in 1931 was General Sir F.S. Maude. He was an officer in the Coldstream Guards studying at the Staff College, who was killed in Baghdad in the First World War. The house was demolished to enable Mr Ray Fairs, the son-in-law of George Doman, to build the new Regal Cinema.

Osnaburgh Parade, the London Road in the 1930s, just outside the new Regal Cinema, advertising the film *Good Night Vienna*. The workmen are busy cutting back the embankment that had been part of the grounds to Osnaburgh House.

The Camberley Drill Hall on the London Road, seen here on the left immediately behind Yorktown Infant School, was built in 1896 by public subscription for the Sandhurst Company of the Berkshire Militia. This privately owned building was transferred to the government at the start of the First World War for general use by all local army personnel. From 1915 it became the HQ of the Surrey Territorial Army 'B' Company of the 5th Battalion of the Queen's. Although primarily built for military use, it was always a place for entertainment, where dances and concerts were held. At the outbreak of the Second World War it was used by the 1st Surrey Battalion of the Home Guard.

'A' Platoon of the Camberley Home Guard, as they marched along the London Road past Osnaburgh Parade, watched by an admiring crowd of local people. Initially known as the Local Defence Volunteers, each company was made up of men either too young or too old for conscription, unfit or in a reserved occupation. The Camberley Company, which was led by Major L.W. Lucas, had at least 160 men and these were split into a number of platoons stationed in the area.

Osnaburgh Parade in the late 1920s or very early '30s, before the demolition of Osnaburgh House, which stood behind this screen of mature trees. The first shop after the trees is the smaller branch of R.P. Over's, which specialised in clothing and drapery. The shop advertising 'Dinners & Teas' is the Coffee Tavern. Beyond these small shops and The Globe public house is R.P. Over's large department store with the spire of the Methodist church rising behind it. The 'Out' sign was used to designate where traffic could leave the parade to join the main traffic flow in the London Road.

The main London Road on a peaceful mid-summer day when it was completely empty of traffic other than one parked car and a dairy cart carrying a milk churn. The Osnaburgh Parade is on the left and the entrance to St Michael's Vicarage is immediately on the right, with the walkway to St Michael's Church branching off beyond it. The cart has a tap at the rear to dispense the milk, and an advertisement proclaiming that the milkman could also provide fresh butter and eggs.

Osnaburgh Parade, the London Road. Mrs W. Searle's Registry Office or Employment Agency was similar to many businesses in the inter-war period that had to offer a range of services to make a living. Apart from her advertised and major trade she also stored bicycles, allowed people to make telephone calls from her premises and sold cigarettes and sweets. The Golden Meadow butter van was probably making a delivery to Mr Harden's grocery store before continuing down the parade towards the Frimley Road.

Acacia Cottage stood behind Barclays Bank on the corner of the London Road and Frimley Road at Yorktown. It was demolished in 1936 to make way for three new shops that were built in the gap between the bank and an existing row of shops. The cottage was probably built in the mid-nineteenth century at a time when the area between Yorktown and the Osnaburgh Hill was being developed and the greatest need was for housing rather than shops. In 1889 the Allen family lived there and from 1896 until the First World War it was occupied by the Pierce family. The last occupant was Mr Fletcher who ran a valet service from the cottage.

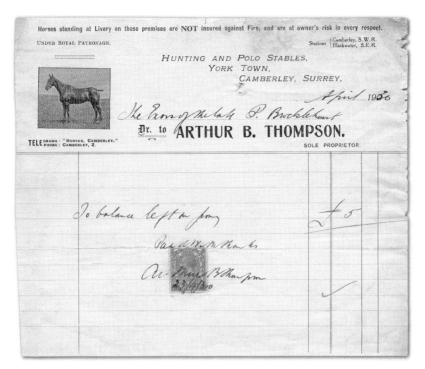

From the foundation of the Royal Military College there would have been a number of livery stables in Yorktown and Camberley. This was the last business of its type to flourish in the town. Owned by Mr A.B. Thompson from at least 1914, it was situated on the corner of the London Road and Victoria Avenue in premises at the rear of the King's Arms, previously occupied for the same purpose by George Doman. In the 1930s Captain R.K. Chiesman ran the business as hunting and polo stables, hiring horses to local residents and army officers.

CAPT. R. K. CHIESMAN

HUNTERS
AND HACKS
FOR HIRE

ENGLISH AND
IRISH HUNTERS
FOR SALE

HUNTERS AND
POLO PONIES
TAKEN AT
LIVERY

HORSE BOX
FOR HIRE

HUNTING   AND   POLO   STABLES
YORKTOWN, CAMBERLEY

Telephone Camberley 450

These buildings had been known for many years as the Victoria Livery Stables, originally owned by George Doman and later by Mr Thompson. They were situated in Yorktown near to Victoria Avenue. When these workmen started demolishing the buildings in 1932 they found evidence of their former use as a chapel. The Wesleyan Methodist chapel opened in Yorktown in 1807 in a tiny room, which was until recently part of the Baptist church premises in Frimley Road. The Methodists sold the chapel to the Baptists in 1819 and moved to this site, a former cottage which they converted by removing the inner walls. They used it until their new chapel on the corner of The Avenue and the London Road opened in 1879.

Agincourt Hall, the London Road, Yorktown, in the 1930s. Agincourt Hall was built in the early part of the nineteenth century, where one of the original owners was Dr Manders who was also captain of the Old Berkshire Volunteer Regiment. The house, which was reputed to be haunted, was a billet for soldiers during the First World War and afterwards a furniture depository. It was purchased by a limited company, chiefly local freemasons who used the house as a meeting place. In May 1929 the Albert Edward Lodge of Freemasons applied for planning permission to build a hall on the west side of the house. Agincourt Hall was designed by H.R. and B.A. Poulter and completed in September 1929. The Hall was built to provide funds for the freemasons and became a major part of Camberley's social life, hosting dinners, receptions, dances and concerts. Facilities at this time included a buffet, lounges, dressing rooms, a Masonic temple and dining hall. In 1930 Mr J.C. Langsdale was the letting agent for the hall he also ran a bootmakers from nearby premises. Later, in the 1960s, it became a popular venue for the top popular music bands of the day such as Rod Stewart, The Merseybeats, John Lee Hooker and others. The hall is still in use today as a music venue.

A delightful 1920s view of a rather overgrown cottage garden shows the rear of the first Frimley National or Church of England School, which was established on the London Road at Yorktown in 1816. Currently forming part of the offices attached to Trends furnishing store, opposite Laundry Lane, it appears to have been erected as a pair of semi-detached cottages, with one half used as classrooms and the other for accommodation. It was built here at a time when the village of Frimley extended from the Blackwater Bridge to the Maultway and south to Mytchett. This was a rapidly growing area, as people moved here with their families to work at the newly erected Royal Military College. When this photograph was taken the premises were used by Mr Lunn, an ironmonger, who let the property to another ironmonger, Mr Oxley, in the mid-1920s.

The Pilgrim's Well or Healing Well at Yorktown was situated behind the shops that line the London Road, near to The Crown public house. It was believed that people travelling the road from London to the west country would stop here to drink the water, which some believed had healing qualities. The well was filled in when a car park was built in the grounds of a factory in Doman Road in the 1960s.

Inside the pipe storage shed at Bates Concrete Manufacturing Company, the London Road, Yorktown, in the early 1930s. The business, known as Eastwoods during the Second World War, was purchased by Trollop & Colls in 1947. It was responsible for the construction of the concrete elephant that still stands today on the site of this former Yorktown factory.

The Three Post Boys antique shop, the London Road, Yorktown, which was formerly a public house, known originally as The Harrow and later as the Three Post Boys. It was the earliest known building in this northern part of the manor of Frimley and was well established by 1667. It abutted the Turnpike Road from London to the west country near Blackwater Bridge. Just east of the building was the Turnpike Gate, where tolls were collected to pay for the upkeep of the road. It is believed it acquired its name from the fact that the postboys, or men who carried the post, from the three counties of Surrey, Berkshire and Hampshire would meet up at this point. The pub closed as licensed premises in December 1913 and was demolished in the 1960s, when a petrol station bearing the same name was built on the site. This has recently been demolished.

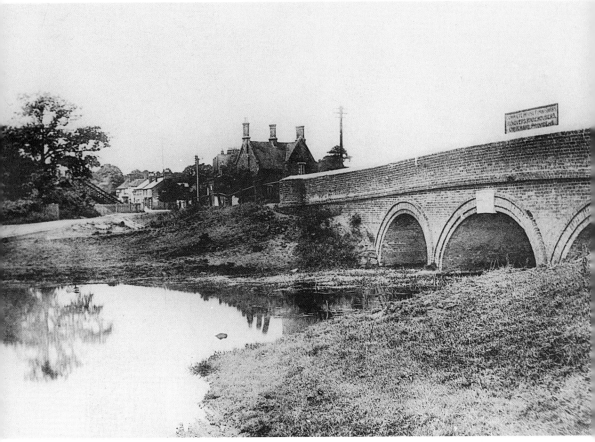

The London to Exeter turnpike road from Yorktown to Blackwater crossed the River Blackwater at Blackwater Bridge, which marks the boundary between Surrey and Hampshire. Wish Stream which flows into it at this point marks the border with Berkshire. There has been a bridge on this site for well over 200 years. A report in the *Reading Mercury and Oxford Gazette*, dated 25 September 1786, stated that magistrates from the three counties held a meeting at the White Hart Inn at Blackwater to consider widening and repairing the bridge. It was suggested that the bridge would be widened to 20ft to the north-west; the parapets on each side to be 5½ft high from the crown of the arches, with a coping of hearts of oak, and to be painted white. This work was then put out to contract: 'Proposals of any person or persons willing to undertake same, are desired to be sealed up, directed and left with Mr William Terry of Yateley before 30 September. A plan is left at the White Hart Inn, Blackwater.' At this time the bridge was 144ft long. The inn can just be seen behind Blackwater station in the foreground. An earlier reference to the bridge occurred in the *Camberley News* on 7 December 1934, which referred to the transcript of an old document where 'John Ridges affidavit touching the Parish of Frimley repairing the highway on the sides of Blackwater Bridge'. Mr Ridges, aged 70, remembers the bridge called Blackwater Bridge and the road either side, particularly the Frimley side which was a muddy and watery place. This recollection was dated 23 January 1727.

3

Streets & Buildings

The centre of Camberley High Street, looking north towards the London Road, with two local photographers and a postcard producer trading within a few yards of each other. John Drew, who lived at Stanton in The Avenue, had two shops selling stationery the other was in the London Road, Yorktown. He produced postcards and street directories, which were printed in Wiltshire, at a printing works where he was a young apprentice in the 1870s and which he purchased in 1907. The Sandhurst Studio, opposite John Drew's, was owned by George E. Clarke, who had originally traded under the name of Beaufort Studios. Beyond the Electric Theatre was the studio of the third photographer, Frederic Robinson, who specialised in high-class portraits of army officers and the local gentry. Nearest the camera on the left is a greengrocer's which was owned by George Hughes.

One of the local post boxes: this one stood on the corner of Portesbury Road and the High Street in Camberley. A 1*d* stamp-dispensing machine is attached to the side. On the opposite side of the road was the Drake & Mount office, where you could order coal. The coal was stored in the goods sidings at Camberley railway station just behind the office. In the 1930s, when this photograph was taken, they were still able to provide corn, seed and animal feed to the few people who were farming in the area. These commodities were stored in their premises at the granary on the corner of Portesbury and Knoll Roads.

A quiet Camberley High Street, probably on a Wednesday afternoon or a Sunday when the shops were closed. It has been decorated for the Silver Jubilee of George V and Queen Mary in 1935 or the Coronation of George VI in 1937. The shops, from left to right, are J.F. Hawkins, men's outfitters; Radio Lobe, owned by Morris Brothers, which sold electrical goods; Frederic Robinson's photographic studio; Chancellor & Sons Estate Agency; Pearson's Café and Boots the Chemist. The only business still trading from the same premises is Chancellor & Sons. Beyond Obelisk Street is James Page's department store, with the striped blinds shading the goods on display in the windows, which from the 1960s until 2005 traded as Allders.

A carnival float mounted by members of Camberley Working Men's Club, depicting the nations of Great Britain and the Dominions, with Britannia seated at centre. The club premises shown here were built in 1907, burned down in 1929 (see overleaf) and were replaced by the present building.

The largest fire to occur in the town centre was at 2 a.m. on the morning of 2 November 1929, when the Camberley Working Men's Club, built in 1907, in Obelisk Street was gutted. The alarm was raised at 2.05 a.m. by PC Rapely who discovered the blaze. The Frimley and Camberley Fire Brigade was first on the scene within ten minutes, but owing to thick fog it took thirty-five minutes for the Frimley Green Section to arrive. The fire was thought to have started in the billiard room but was too intense to control, so efforts were concentrated on saving the adjacent cottages, the old Congregational church and Soames Hairdressing shop. The roof of Mrs Soames's house in Cross Street caught fire, but this was put out before significant damage occurred. Damage to the club was estimated at £7,000. The fire was the third disturbing incident to occur at the club in the previous week. The first was a small fire in the bar room, on 25 October, which was quickly extinguished; on the following Wednesday £40 was stolen from the safe in the bar room. There was a body of local opinion that the fire was started deliberately, although nothing was ever proved. *Below:* Camberley Working Men's Club fire at its height.

The Working Men's Club was subsequently rebuilt on the same site and opened by the President, Len Ellis, on 31 December 1930. This is the new club, decorated for a royal celebration.

The bar area in the new club.

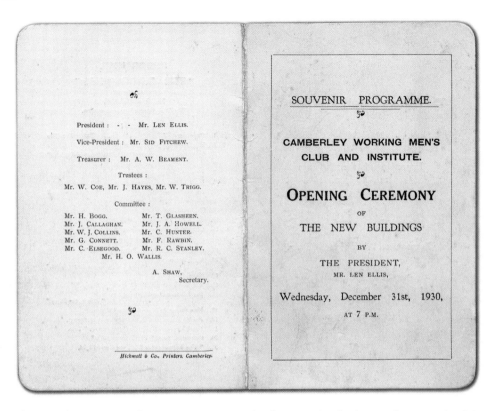

President : - - Mr. LEN ELLIS.

Vice-President : Mr. SID FITCHEW.

Treasurer : Mr. A. W. BEAMENT.

Trustees :

Mr. W. COE, Mr. J. HAYES, Mr. W. TRIGG.

Committee :

Mr. H. BOGG.　　　Mr. T. GLASHEEN.
Mr. J. CALLAGHAN.　Mr. J. A. HOWELL.
Mr. W. J. COLLINS.　Mr. C. HUNTER.
Mr. G. CONNETT.　　Mr. F. RAWBIN.
Mr. C. ELSEGOOD.　　Mr. R. C. STANLEY.
Mr. H. O. WALLIS.

A. SHAW,
Secretary.

Hickmott & Co., Printers, Camberley.

SOUVENIR PROGRAMME.

CAMBERLEY WORKING MEN'S
CLUB AND INSTITUTE.

OPENING CEREMONY

OF

THE NEW BUILDINGS

BY

THE PRESIDENT,

MR. LEN ELLIS,

Wednesday, December 31st, 1930,

AT 7 P.M.

The opening ceremony Souvenir Programme for the new Camberley Working Men's Club.

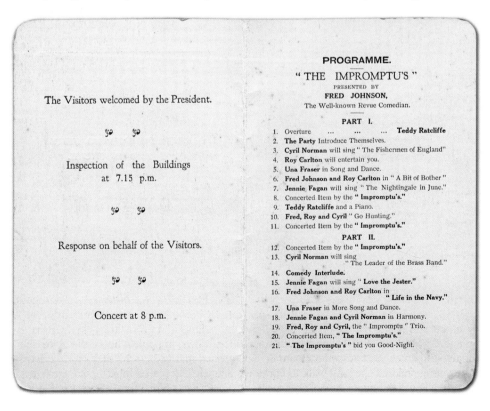

The Visitors welcomed by the President.

Inspection of the Buildings
at 7.15 p.m.

Response on behalf of the Visitors.

Concert at 8 p.m.

PROGRAMME.

"THE IMPROMPTU'S"

PRESENTED BY

FRED JOHNSON,

The Well-known Revue Comedian.

PART I.

1. Overture　...　...　...　**Teddy Ratcliffe**
2. **The Party** Introduce Themselves.
3. **Cyril Norman** will sing " The Fishermen of England"
4. **Roy Carlton** will entertain you.
5. **Una Fraser** in Song and Dance.
6. **Fred Johnson and Roy Carlton** in " A Bit of Bother "
7. **Jennie Fagan** will sing " The Nightingale in June."
8. Concerted Item by the " **Impromptu's.**"
9. **Teddy Ratcliffe** and a Piano.
10. **Fred, Roy and Cyril** " Go Hunting."
11. Concerted Item by the " **Impromptu's.**"

PART II.

12. Concerted Item by the " **Impromptu's.**"
13. **Cyril Norman** will sing
" The Leader of the Brass Band."
14. **Comedy Interlude.**
15. **Jennie Fagan** will sing " **Love the Jester.**"
16. **Fred Johnson and Roy Carlton** in
" **Life in the Navy.**"
17. **Una Fraser** in More Song and Dance.
18. **Jennie Fagan and Cyril Norman** in Harmony.
19. **Fred, Roy and Cyril,** the " Impromptu " Trio.
20. Concerted Item, " **The Impromptu's.**"
21. " **The Impromptu's** " bid you Good-Night.

This is the earliest photograph in a sequence that records the gradual redevelopment of the south side of Obelisk Street. It shows the shop on the corner of Obelisk Street and School Lane with the nine cottages that stood between School Lane and the Prince of Wales public house. The owner of the shop was a jack-of-all-trades businessman, William Henry Soane, who was a plumber in 1907 and had become a gentleman's hairdresser by the time this photograph was taken in about 1926. In the next of the series the shop is being used as a laundry, and as Mr and Mrs Soane were resident here until at least 1938 they obviously felt there was more money to be made from a laundry than either plumbing or hairdressing.

Looking down the narrow School Lane that connected Obelisk Street and Princess Street with the Camberley Infant and Junior School on the left behind the railings and Cross Street on the right. At the far end of the lane the large building facing the entrance is the Brown Jug public house in Princess Street. The school, initially known as the Camberley Board School, opened in 1887 on the site just behind this shop to save the very young children the long walk to Yorktown School. The central building, containing classrooms and the school hall, and the junior school classrooms nearer Princess Street were all erected in 1901.

Obelisk Street on a sunny day in the 1930s. The buildings on the right up to School Lane were due to be demolished to make way for Camberley's first car park. Next to the new Working Men's Club is White's newly built garage workshop, which was built after the demolition of the non-conformist chapel that had stood there since the 1880s. The first of the semi-detached houses in the row used to be the home of John Whitehead, a Crimean veteran who was the last local survivor of the Charge of the Light Brigade.

No. 29 Obelisk Street (left), home of Crimea War veteran John Whitehead. He was born in 1826 and enlisted in the 4th Light Dragoons in 1846. The *Camberley News* report stated that he was present at the Battle of Alma. Subsequently, as one of the six hundred of Lord Cardigan's Light Brigade, he rode through the Russian Valley of Death. In the charge his horse was shot from under him, but Mr Whitehead escaped and successfully returned to the British lines. He was also at Inkerman and the Siege of Sebastopol. When he was discharged from the army in 1871 he came to live in Obelisk Street, which was his home until his death in 1915. The body of John Whitehead was received at St Tarcisius's Church by Father Twomey. The following day the funeral cortège gathered in the London Road with an escort band from the Royal Military College. The Royal Engineers formed the firing party and escort, while the Army Service Corps provided the gun carriage on which the coffin was conveyed to St Michael's churchyard where he was buried. The graveside service was conducted by Father Twomey.

John Whitehead (1826–1915), Crimea War veteran.

Frimley & Camberley Urban District Council purchased nine houses in this area of Obelisk Street in 1938 at a cost of £2,910. They were demolished later that year to make way for the first car park in Camberley. This photograph shows nos 21 to 25 minus their slates and with what appears to be floorboards erected as a temporary barrier. In January 1939 the borough surveyor reported that the highest tender for the purchase of the materials from these houses was only £32 15s, as there did not appear to be any demand for them.

Upper Charles Street, which ran parallel with the London Road in Camberley, on a rather bleak day in the late 1920s or early '30s, with the garden of Mr Knight of Lower Charles Street on the left. Beyond the garden are the fir trees in the back garden of Staff House, which stood on the London Road and was owned by Harry Doman. He also owned all the houses in Upper Charles Street, which he rented out for £17 a year. The alleyway at the end of the street led to Park Street with Wells Bakery on the right of the narrow gap. The houses were some of the first built by Captain Charles Raleigh Knight when he laid out this new town in 1862. Harry and Julia Doman purchased them from his son Henry in 1894. The site was cleared in the early 1960s and currently forms part of the Atrium development.

This pair of single-storey houses next to the fire station was known as Avenue Cottages. They were probably the first dwellings built in The Avenue at a time when it was known as Plantation Road. They were occupied in the early 1930s by Mr Yate and Mr Hammond. They pre-date the fire station, which was built in 1901 at a cost of £150. The cottages are typical of the small dwellings built to house working-class families in the mid-nineteenth century. They generally consisted of a living room, one or two small bedrooms and a scullery and wash-house at the rear.

This imposing entrance is to one of the largest estates in Park Road, Camberley, in the 1930s, with the well-established avenue of trees that led to the house, Brackenhurst, one of several houses built in this area between 1870 and 1890. The first occupier of the house was Major-General Abbot Anderson, a professor of topography at the Royal Military College who became so well known in the town that a fountain was erected in his memory and paid for by public subscription. This fountain currently stands just outside the Arena Leisure Centre in the London Road Recreation Ground. In the 1930s Brackenhurst was occupied by General Sir Arthur Wynne.

The original lodge, which stood at the entrance to the Watchetts Estate in Park Road, Camberley, just before the sale of the estate in 1928. Through the gates, next to the Sadler & Baker sale sign, was one of the main carriageways leading to the house, which had been planted with deciduous trees. In 1924, when the estate was owned by local poulterer and fishmonger Nicholas Verran, the road was widened and strengthened and a sewer installed by Harvey Percy Estates Ltd. It appears that Verran went no further with any development. It was not until after he died and his estate was sold off that any houses were built in the newly named Parkway. The first four houses were erected by J.R. McLean Keil in 1931.

The house which replaced Watchetts Lodge in Park Road was built for Mr Ralph Tolley by local builder George Hoskins in 1928. Named Locarno, it stands on the corner of Park Road and Parkway. Mr Tolley was a baker who owned a business with his brother on the London Road in Camberley.

The Poplars in the Frimley Road, also known as Park Lodge, was built for Captain Henry Raleigh Knight, the eldest son of the man who laid out the town of Camberley. It was let to a succession of military men, including Major Francis Coningsby Hammond Clarke in 1882 and Lieutenant-Colonel John Sutton Rothwell in 1889. In the 1930s it was the home of Major A.J. Saunders. It was vacant when the Second World War broke out in September 1939 and the building was adapted as a casualty clearing and cleansing station. Postwar, with the advent of the National Health Service in 1948, it housed a baby clinic, dentist and inoculation centre. It was demolished in the 1980s and the Frimley Road Health Centre now stands on the site.

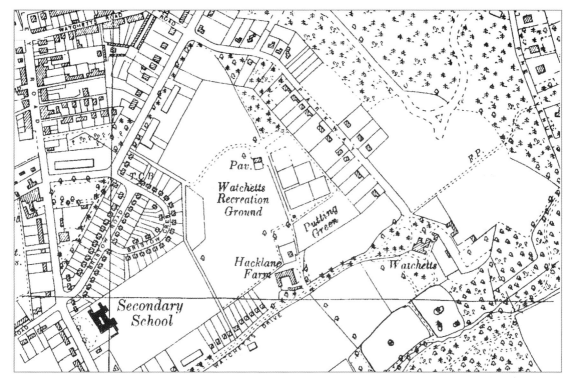

Watchetts Estate, 1934.

An avenue of Wellingtonias in Watchetts Drive. This splendid double row of Wellingtonias was planted along the road leading to Watchetts House from the Frimley Road. The house was erected for Major Spring, the brother-in-law of Captain Charles Raleigh Knight who lived nearby at Tekel's Castle. The estate was laid out in the early 1860s and this new lane replaced an earlier one, which was situated north of Hack Lane Farm. This established a more direct route to the Gothic-style mansion, with a further row of trees close to the lodge, which was erected at the Frimley Road entrance to the estate. There was also a further double row of these trees planted at Heatherside at about the same time, to provide a wind and frost break for the tender plants growing at Heatherside Nursery.

Watchetts House from the sale catalogue when the house was sold by auction in May 1928. It was described as a 'magnificent house' with an 'entrance hall intersected by stone Gothic arches supported on marble pilasters'. It had nine bedrooms and the five reception rooms included a billiard room.

Opposite, top: Watchetts House, parklands and lake.

Opposite, bottom: The stable block to the Watchetts estate. Watchetts House was built for Major Spring in about 1862. He sold it to James Herbert Butler Hollings, often referred to as Squire Hollings, whose wife was the sister of the composer and suffragette Dame Ethel Smyth. His only son was killed in action in the First World War and when he died his daughter sold the estate to Nicholas Verran. During 1928 and 1929 two auctions were held to sell off the land in third of an acre building plots along what is now known as Watchetts Drive and Parkway. The stable block was described in the sale catalogue as consisting of a large coach or motor house, a six-stall stable with two loose boxes and a harness room, and a three-bedroomed cottage to house the coachman or chauffeur.

The old barn which used to stand in the grounds of Hack Lane or Axe Lane Farm, Frimley. The farm had been one of the demesne farms of the manor of Frimley, that is, a farm owned by the manor and let out to tenants. It was one of only two farms, the other being Bristow Farm, north of the village of Frimley until after the Enclosure Act of 1801. At the rear of the barns are a row of Wellingtonia trees planted in Watchetts Drive, which was laid out in the 1860s as one of the routes to Watchetts House.

Hack Lane or Axe Lane Farm, Frimley, which stands between Watchetts Drive and Watchetts Recreation Ground, is one of the few old buildings left in the Camberley area. Much altered since the Second World War, it was originally on a trackway, which crossed the heathland from the Jolly Farmer to Bristow Farm, where there was a small bridge across the Blackwater River into Hampshire. This route used to be north of the farmhouse through what is now the recreation ground.

Harcourt House Hotel, Frimley Road, Camberley, was situated just off the London Road opposite the William IV public house. It was formerly a private dwelling, built in about 1870. Many large Victorian houses in the area were converted into hotels or, alternatively, to office or light industrial use. Harcourt House was purchased by Mr Keil in 1930 and let to Mrs Brook as a hotel from 1930 to 1934. The hotel had an extensive garden, a sun lounge, gas fires in all bedrooms, and produced its own vegetables, poultry and eggs. When the hotel was demolished a small housing development was built, known as Sullivan Road.

An advertisement for Kingsclear Hotel, Park Road, Camberley. Kingsclear House was built in 1885 next to Brackenhurst in Park Road, for Colonel Cooper-King. Just before its conversion for use as a hotel it had been the home of Sir Percy Newson, President of the Bank of Bengal, Governor of the Imperial Bank of India and an MP for Warwickshire. In the early 1950s it was purchased by Hampshire cricketer and local architect Mr Maurice Lawson who converted it for use as a hotel. In 1954 it was adapted for what was then known as the Kingsclear Old Folk's Home.

Kingsclear Old Folk's Home, Park Road, Camberley.

The Camberley Court Hotel, formally Firlands House, was bordered by Gordon Road, Park Road and Firlands Avenue, and was adjacent to the Elmhurst Ballet School. The house was purchased by Maurice Lawson, an architect and brother-in-law of James Page who owned the department store in the High Street. Mr Lawson converted the house into a hotel. The facility, to quote its advertising, was 'the finest residential hotel in the district', with every modern convenience, including tennis courts and separate lock-up garages. Many large houses in the area were adapted during the Second World War for military use. Firlands was used as a recuperation hospital during the First World War; the patients wore blue uniforms. The more able patients could play croquet or bowls, or just relax in the conservatory or in the large garden. The hotel has since been demolished and replaced with a block of flats.

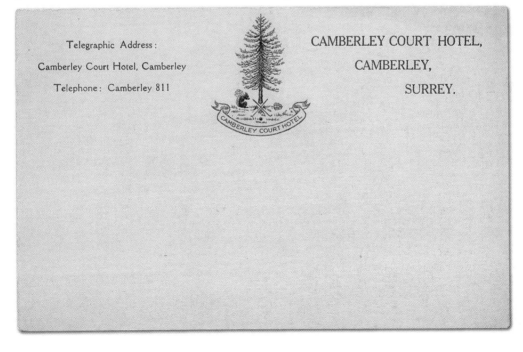

Telegraphic Address:

Camberley Court Hotel, Camberley

Telephone: Camberley 811

CAMBERLEY COURT HOTEL,

CAMBERLEY,

SURREY.

A view of the Portsmouth Road at the junction with Crawley Hill to the right and Prior Road to the left. The car on the main road is travelling from the Frimley direction towards Bagshot. The sign on the right was erected by the Waverley Court Estate, which owned most of the land from Portsmouth Road to Church Hill, all part of the former Frimley Park Estate. The land was purchased by a local firm of estate agents, Hankinson & Son, for its client Mr T.D. Edwards in 1892. In 1895 Waverley Court and The Holt were the only two houses to have been built. Waverley Drive, Castle Road and Connaught Road were all laid out by 1907. Between 1907 and 1913 the number of houses built adjacent to these roads had increased from eleven to thirty-eight. As can be seen from the prominence of this sign there were still large plots up for sale in the 1930s.

The entrance to the Beaufront Estate in the Portsmouth Road, Camberley, in 1931, when the old lodge next to the gate was referred to as the 'old shooting lodge'. Originally known as Maywood, the land on which it was built was sold by Thomas Boys to James Flexman, a builder, in 1887. The name Beaufront was used from 1920 when the new owner, Miss Rimington, re-named the girls boarding school she purchased from Miss Carr, which had been established there in 1907. During the Second World War the school moved to other premises in the Portsmouth Road and the house was requisitioned for military use. It was here that Princess Elizabeth was based when she joined the ATS in 1944.

Frimley Park when it was the home of Theodore Alexander and Chariclia Ralli, in the 1930s. They moved into the former Frimley manor house in 1920. At the onset of the Second World War they allowed one wing of the house to be used as a maternity home for local mothers and another was utilised as a convalescent home for injured officers.

4

Transport & Uniform

The first motorised ambulance in Camberley replaced an earlier horse-drawn version in the 1920s. At the time it was known as the Frimley and Camberley Motor Ambulance and it was affiliated to the Order of St John of Jerusalem and the British Red Cross. Before the introduction of the National Health Service each patient making use of the ambulance had to pay a fee of 1s 3d a mile. The ambulances were kept at H. Solomon's Garage in the High Street, Camberley.

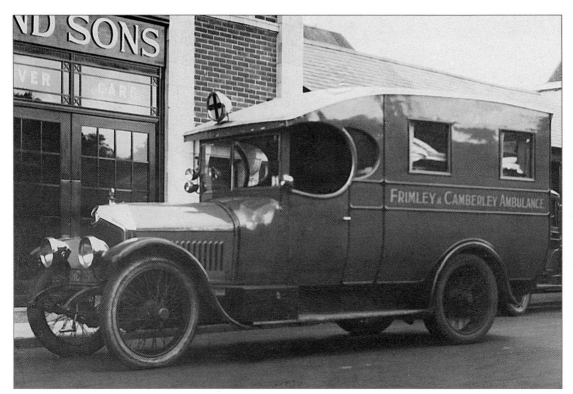

Camberley's second ambulance outside H. Solomon's Garage. Mr Walter Mountford of Park Street drove the second and third versions. Below he can be seen standing by the door of the third ambulance outside the garage, with St George's Church just visible behind him. Walter Mountford also drove Solomon's breakdown truck.

Mr Albin Edward Jupp lived at
Clematis Cottage, Moorland Road,
Camberley. He was the first
ambulance officer for the area
and preceded Mr Mountford.
Mr Jupp was also quartermaster
for the British Red Cross Society.
He died on 13 July 1929.

Mr Lansley in the early 1930s, with the last horse-drawn cab for hire in Camberley, which he kept at the rear of J. Smith & Son greengrocery shop in the London Road. The original horse-drawn cab service in the area was founded by Mr McLaughlin of the King's Arms public house in Yorktown, who had a stable block at the back of his premises. Another publican, Mr George Doman of the William IV in Frimley Road, set up a rival service. The bus office was at the rear of the Duke of York hotel and the service ran from Blackwater to Camberley railway station. Known as Doman's Sixpenny Bus, it was drawn by a pair of horses and the drivers were Mr Kirkpatrick and Mr J. Farr.

This 1903 De Dion Swift car was purchased for £10 in 1930 by Herman Solomon, founder of Solomon & Sons garage, which stood in the High Street in Camberley. Here, one of his sons, Gerald, is pictured inside the garage workshop warmly clad and ready to take to the road on the London to Brighton annual run. They competed in this run from 1931 until at least 1974 (except during the Second World War), and in this time the car only suffered one major breakdown.

The wedding of Fireman Reginald Poulter took place at the Baptist chapel in Frimley Road, Camberley, in July 1934. The bride and groom are seen leaving the chapel under an archway of axes and then sitting on the front seat of a new Morris Commercial Tender, which was purchased in December 1933. Reg and his father William were both members of the Frimley and Camberley Fire Brigade.

The Surrey Border and Camberley 10¼in Miniature Railway was the ambitious brainchild of merchant banker Mr A.D. Kinloch. It was preceded by the Foxhill's Miniature Railway (MR) and the Farnborough Miniature Railway (FMR). The Foxhill's MR was inspired and built in late 1935 by Mr H.C. Bullock, a practical engineer and innovator, who intended to use the line as a showcase for his engines to demonstrate them to potential customers. The single-track line ran from Foxhill station, situated in a field close to the present Farnborough Sixth Form College, to the intended terminus at Lye Copse (now a housing estate). At this stage, and purely by chance, Mr Kinloch became involved. He was a wealthy banker with a passion for steam and met Mr Bullock on several occasions, when he was able to try out engines on the new track and eventually ordered one of his own. With Kinloch's wealth and enthusiasm, he formed a partnership with Bullock to expand and extend the line at Lye Copse and add a new terminus near the Fox Inn, Hawley. At the end of May 1936, although still not fully operational, it opened to the public, and was a great success. It was reported in the local press that over 4,000 passengers were carried in the first two weeks. In January 1937 the line was re-branded the Farnborough Miniature Railway to reach a wider market. At this time relations between Bullock and Kinloch were becoming increasingly strained, in part because of financial matters. Early in 1937 Bullock decided he'd had enough and took two tank engines – No. 3007 and No. 3008 – a few coaches and sufficient rail and built his own line at California-in-England, near Eversley, Hampshire. Unfortunately, the strain was too much and Mr Bullock passed away on 20 November 1937.

Kinloch continued to run the FMR himself, extending the line further and increasing the coaching stock. However, despite considerable advertising, the enterprise had still not broken even. More passengers were needed, but the railway was difficult to find and there were land problems with the local council. It was at this point that Kinloch decided to move the railway to an ideal site enclosed by the Aldershot to Ascot line,

Farnborough Green station.

woodland and the River Blackwater. A new terminus was to be built by the side of the A325 road, close to the Southern Railway station at Frimley. Work began on the Surrey Border and Camberley Railway (SB&CR) early in 1938. This was a large and ambitious business enterprise, which was expected to be profitable. The railway was initially to have four stations: one at Frimley (Farnborough Green), one half-way at Watchetts Wood, one at Vale Road, Yorktown (Camberley), then over the river to a terminus at Blackwater (this was never built). An extra intermediate station at Cove Wood was added. The main station at Farnborough Green was most impressive with three concrete island platforms, two carriage sidings, a locomotive run-around, most of which was under cover (see page 68). The timber-built buildings consisted of an entrance hall, booking hall, large waiting room and stationmaster's office. A typical ride from Farnborough Green station would take you past the signal-box on the left, the turntable and engine shed, then over a level

Surrey Border and Camberley Railway programme and timetable.

crossing, alongside the River Blackwater, then into the trees at Cove Wood station. You could alight here and walk through the flower-lined woods. From Cove Wood, the line ran through open pasture adjacent to the Aldershot–Ascot line, to Watchetts Wood station (see page 72). The last section of line to Camberley station was completed after the official opening and was built on the site of a rubbish tip. The station had a single, long platform with a booking office at the end, a long carriage siding and turntable. The photograph on page 72 shows Moorland Road behind the station. Surrey Avenue also bordered the terminus and Avenue Sucy was initially known as Border Avenue.

The SB&CR was officially opened on Saturday 23 July 1938 by Graham Moffatt, the fat boy from Will Hay's classic film *Oh, Mr Porter!* A summer timetable was introduced and a daily service was run at 10.30 a.m. from Farnborough Green to arrive at Camberley at 10.45 a.m. and back to Farnborough by 11.05 a.m. This was an hourly service until 2.30 p.m. then half-hourly until 9.30 p.m. Additional trains were run at weekends. Fares were 1s 6d return; special excursions on Sundays and Bank Holidays after 6.30 p.m. were only 1s return.

Some of the engines used on the railway were *Edward VIII*, Garratt No. 4012 and No. 4013, *Western Queen*, *Coronation* (driven by Graham Moffatt on the opening day), tank locomotive No. 3008 *Silver Jubilee*, *Wendy*, *The Empress* and *Harvester*.

To pull in the crowds, special events and features were frequently held, and camp sites and picnic sites were set up along the line. There was also an illustrated booklet entitled *An Illustrated Description, Timetable and Particulars of Cheap Travelling Facilities, Camping and Picnicking*; all details were available at the café and shops on the premises. In the autumn the Mount Olivet Circus set up in Watchetts Wood.

However, all this was to be of no avail, because on 3 September 1939 war was declared and the railway closed forever. This may have been a blessing in disguise as fresh money would certainly have been required for the railway to have survived.

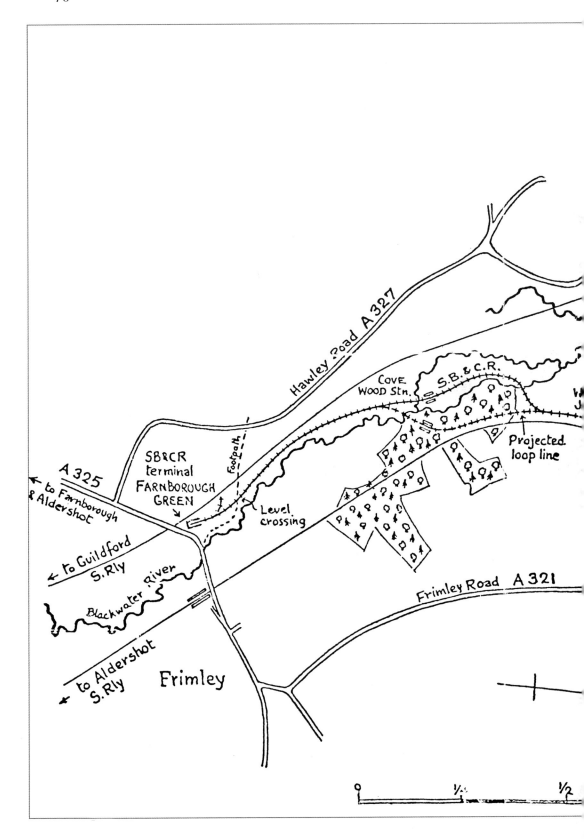

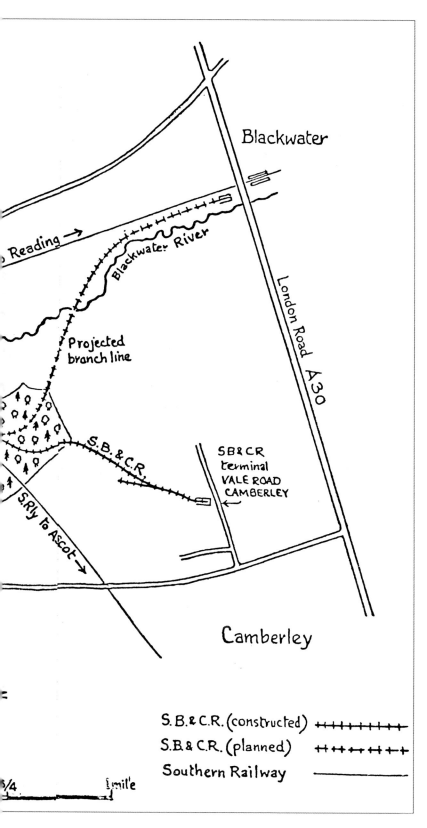

Blackwater

Reading →

Blackwater River

Projected branch line

London Road A30

S.B.& C.R.

SB&CR terminal
VALE ROAD
CAMBERLEY

S.Rly to Ascot →

Camberley

S.B.& C.R. (constructed) ++++++++++

S.B.& C.R. (planned) ++ +++++ ++ ++

Southern Railway ——————

¾   ½ mile

SB&CR layout,
April 1938.

Camberley station, SB&CR.

Watchetts Wood station, SB&CR.

A typical newspaper advertisement for 1938 extolling the virtues of the SB&CR.

THIS WEEK'S NEWS OF THE RAILWAYS

WE GIVE YOU A SQUARE DEAL!

HOLIDAY SEASON FEATURE AT THE

Surrey Border & Camberley Railway

Farnborough Green Station
Farnborough, Hants.

Camberley Station
Camberley, Surrey

DECEMBER 26th FOR ONE WEEK

A RETURN RIDE AND A
TRIP TO THE TOY FAIR

(Fares from 1/-, children half-price)

including a

PRESENT FROM FATHER CHRISTMAS

BRING YOUR CHILDREN TO THE FINEST MINIATURE RAILWAY IN THE COUNTRY

Traction engine accident, the London Road, Camberley. A Foden 6-ton Steam Wagon YK 6022, belonging to the Union Cartage Co. Ltd, No. 11874, lost control and smashed through the railings on the London Road adjacent to the recreation ground. The wagon was made near Sandbach, Cheshire, and was supplied new to the Union Cartage Co. by the London agent, H.C. Bauley & Co., in July 1925 as part of its fleet. It was used for hauling frozen meat from Smithfield Market.

Construction of Camberley's new car park in 1939. The land in Obelisk Street was cleared by December 1938, but there was quite a delay before work commenced. In July 1939 they were still laying the drainage pipes. Here the bays for parking are being laid out in the autumn of 1939. The total cost of the building works, which included the erection of a toilet block and a car park attendant's ticket office, was £3,660. The cottages in the background are 14 to 36 Cross Street.

Mr J.W. Broadbent, car park attendant.

Camberley Car Park was officially opened on 22 November 1939 by Lieutenant-Colonel L.W. Lucas DSO, Chairman of the Frimley & Camberley Urban District Council. Those attending were Mrs Dorothy Worsley, Mr J. Appleton, Major W. Craig, Captain T. Loman (Chairman of the Highways Committee), Mr P. Marshment, Captain J. Newland and Mr R. Parsons. There was only a small public attendance at the opening ceremony. Mr Lucas said in his speech that in recent years congestion in the High Street and shopping area had warranted the building of the car park and it would be a valuable amenity for the town. This car park was on the south side of Obelisk Street and had provision for eighty-one cars and about forty motorcycles. Public conveniences were also provided and were open day and night. The first person to drive into the car park was Alderman David Sparvell. The six houses which were demolished to make way for the car park cost the council £2,910. It was reported in the local press, on 8 December 1939, that an ultimatum had been issued by Captain Loman that unless the car park was used street parking regulations would come into force. Mr Parsons reported that on the previous Saturday there were only 8 cars in the car park but 28 cars in Obelisk Street and over 100 cars in the High Street. It was suggested that the car park should be free until 1 p.m. Only twenty-nine cars used the car park in the first week. Mr J.W. Broadbent was the car park attendant, who earned the princely sum of £2 10s 8d per week.

The opening of Camberley Car Park, showing the new toilets, car park and attendant block.

The car park's first customer, Alderman David Sparvell.

Captain Harold James Cox (left), who lived at Brakenfell, Church Hill, Camberley, had a long and distinguished career in the Frimley and Camberley Fire Brigade (FCFB). He was an architect by profession with an office in the High Street, Camberley, but spent his early professional years in the Royal Engineers from 1907 until his retirement in 1922 when he held the rank of Captain. He became Chief Fire Officer of the FCFB at the end of June 1923. In August 1935 he was presented with the King's Silver Jubilee Medal for services as Chief Fire Officer. Captain Cox was highly respected by the local community and by the men under his command. He was instrumental in upgrading the brigade's equipment and improving safety and efficiency on a regular basis. He was Officer in Charge of Camberley during the period of the National Fire Service from August 1941 to March 1948 and served with the Surrey Fire Brigade from April 1948 until his retirement at the end of 1950. He was presented with the King's Fire Service Medal by the Lord Lieutenant of Surrey on 22 July 1950 at a ceremony at Guildford fire station. He died in Frimley Hospital on 29 August 1959, aged 78, and was buried in St Michael's churchyard on the London Road.

Surrey Joint Special Constabulary D Division, Camberley. D Division was based at Camberley and in the 1930s, when this Christmas card was sent, a number of well-known local men were members of the division. In 1932 Mr Frank Stallwood was their leader but he died in 1937 and Mr A.H. Coventry, who lived in Gordon Road, took over the leadership. Others who served at this time were Percy White of White's Garage, Captain John Newland, who lived at The Warren in Frimley, and Section Leader Mr D. Barrie of Yorktown. Of the men in this group, only C.E. Smith has been identified, and is seated in the centre of the front row. He lived in Charles Street and worked for photographer's Marshall & Son.

Surrey Joint Special Constabulary
D Division Camberley

Wednesday sub-section wish you a
Happy Christmas

The funeral of ex-Fireman Shaver Tomms passing by Dr Twort's house, Hurstwood, the London Road, Camberley, June 1931. Fireman Tomms, who was known as the father of the brigade, had joined the Volunteer Fire Service as a call boy. In the days before a bell system a call boy would run around to the homes or places of work of volunteer fireman informing them that their services were needed by giving three blasts on a whistle. The buildings behind the cortège are the Staff Hotel and George Wakeman's store on the corner of Park Street.

The funeral of Engineer Officer Herman Solomon took place in June 1935. His coffin, with his fire brigade axe, belt and helmet, were laid on the new Frimley Green Morris Commercial Tender that had been used the year before to convey Fireman Reginald Poulter and his wife from their wedding. The main tender was followed by two from the Camberley and Windlesham Fire Brigades that were banked high with floral tributes. The police halted the traffic and Captain Cox led the mourners along the High Street, down Princess Street and Park Street. As they reached the Frimley Road those attending the funeral service climbed on to the tenders for the drive to St Peter's Church in Frimley. His grave bears the inscription 'His Last Call – 28 June 1935' beside a fireman's helmet made of marble.

FRIMLEY AND CAMBERLEY URBAN DISTRICT COUNCIL

SPITFIRE FUND

Dear Sir or Madam,

By his gift of £5,000 to buy one Spitfire Mr. A. A. Ralli has set an example of true public spiritedness to the rest of this Urban District. Not only is it an example but also a challenge. I feel sure that the residents of the Urban District will agree with me that we can show our appreciation of this patriotic gesture in no better way than by raising a further £5,000 for the same purpose.

The Council has, therefore, unanimously decided to inaugurate a Fund with the object of raising £5,000 to provide a ''Frimley and Camberley'' Spitfire.

Please give quickly and generously.

Contributions may be paid into any Bank in the District or forwarded to me at the address below. Every contribution will be acknowledged in ''Camberley News.''

T. LOMAN,
Chairman of the Council.

Municipal Buildings,
Camberley.
23rd August, 1940.

FRIMLEY AND CAMBERLEY SPITFIRE FUND

I enclose a contribution of £   :   s.   d. to the above Fund.

Signed

Address

To the Chairman of the Council,
Municipal Buildings, Camberley.

Spitfire Fund for 1945. Early in the Second World War Lord Beaverbrook came up with the idea of encouraging individuals and towns to sponsor an aircraft. This presentation aircraft would then bear the name of the town or donor. The price for having a Spitfire named was set at £5,000, although the true cost of this aircraft at the time was almost £12,000. Supermarine Spitfire Mark IIa P8429 was named *Frimley & Camberley* after £5,135 was raised by public subscription. Built at Vickers Armstrong, Castle Bromwich, the Spitfire entered service on 24 May 1941 carrying out day-to-day fighter and convoy duties until it was assigned to 61 Operational Training Unit at Montford Bridge, where it was destroyed in an aerial collision with another Spitfire on 8 April 1943. Theodore Alexander Ralli of Frimley Park House was the first local man to purchase a Spitfire and many believe he was the first in the country. Originally from Liverpool, where his family were in the cotton-broking industry, he moved to the 140-acre Frimley Park Estate in 1920 and became well known as a benefactor of local causes. Other schemes were used to encourage donations for equipment, such as tanks, and towns were also asked to adopt vessels and provide comforts for the crews.

5

Retail

Cousins & Son, greengrocer, High Street, Camberley in the 1920s. Henry Albert
Cousins, a fruiterer and greengrocer, was established in the area at the turn of the
nineteenth century. In 1901/2 he had a shop in the Frimley Road near the Duke of
York hotel, which he rented from the Baptist church. By 1903 he had purchased a
shop in the High Street, Camberley, on the corner of St George's Road, where he sold
fruit, vegetables and flowers; he was also an agent for Sale & Son's Seeds.
The business flourished here for over eighty years, then the lease ran out and the
Cousins moved to smaller premises in Park Street. The shop finally closed in March
1991 with the proposed redevelopment of Park Street. Today, sadly, there are no
greengrocers left in Camberley.

Ernest Victor Lomas-Smith opened his electrical shop in Camberley High Street in June 1926. Every week at this time there was an article in the *Camberley News* entitled 'Wireless Notes' by 'Jack Broadcaster', giving information on the opening of new masts, extra stations and programmes, and tips on how to improve the sound quality of your wireless. Mr Lomas-Smith had taken over premises owned by Mr Lenthall, where bicycles had been made and repaired from early in the century. He also had a business in Bagshot in 1932. This impressive display of batteries was probably sponsored by Ever Ready as a sales promotion for torch, cycle and radio batteries. Today this site is occupied by the HSBC Bank.

One of the last people working a forge in Camberley, mid-1920s. It is believed that the man at work is Mr Bartlett, the father of Ivy Potten, who recalled visiting him and watching him work in his forge in her book *Looking Back in Longing*: 'Proceeding along an alleyway, which led to the High Street, we must stop and meet my father at work, for this is where his forge is situated. Even before we get near we are aware of the particular smells of smoke and horses, and we can hear the special ringing tones of the hammer on the anvil. . . . The brilliant sparks would fly like stars from his hammer . . . I would shudder as the shoe reached the hoof still sizzling, and was hammered into place, with quick, sure blows from the hammer.'

J.F. Hawkins outside his gentlemen's outfitter's shop, which stood in Camberley High Street from 1902 until the late 1980s. James Frederick Hawkins, who was born in Staines in 1865, was apprenticed to Peter Robinson, one of the top boys' outfitter's in the country, which was situated in Oxford Street, London. He was at Peter Robinson until his move to Camberley in 1902. His shop specialised in boys' school outfits for public and preparatory schools all over the country, as well as many local schools. Officers serving abroad would send their sons to him to be kitted out before they went to Eton, Harrow, Marlborough or Wellington. He also supplied Indian and colonial outfits for officers posted abroad from the Royal Military College and Staff College. A member of the staff interviewed in 1977 remembered that 'Indian aristocrats often visited Camberley and one of these was Maharajah Ranji Singh, who came complete with 30 servants – there was even one especially for the parrot. He hired a fleet of cars, complete with chauffeurs, which drove in a cavalcade through the town. Another extravagant customer was Mr Vanderspar from Ceylon who took over Mulroy House, he also had thirty servants. All the servants were sent to be outfitted at Hawkins in grey flannel uniforms, consisting of trousers and tunics.' Mr Hawkins was also one of the founder members of the Chamber of Trade.

Sanders family butcher, showing a nice display of meat, in the 1930s. The shop was situated at 40 Park Street. The sign on the bicycle was for A.G. Hendin, who owned the shop during the First World War. Before this the shop was also a butcher's owned by C. & W. Theobald, who may have been the first occupants. Next door to Sanders was Russell & Son Fishmonger and Poulterer (left) and Stokes & Sons Dairy (right). Russell's closed in September 1974 and was the last old-fashioned wet fish shop in Camberley where one could also buy fresh poultry and game.

A view of Park Street in Camberley, in the late 1930s, looking north from Park Road, with Gordon Road to the left and Middle Gordon Road to the right. A new purpose-built post office on the corner of Middle Gordon Road was erected in 1911 for Mr Love, the sub-postmaster, who had started work in Camberley in the building diagonally opposite his new shop. This earlier shop, the first building on the left in this view, opened in 1899 to save customers a walk to the main post office in the London Road.

The family grocer's on the corner of Park Road and Middle Gordon Road was owned by Mr A.N. Mercer in 1935, then by Mr W.B. Trowbridge, who ran the business throughout the Second World War.

The old post office in the London Road, Camberley, after it was vacated in 1937 for the move to new premises further along the London Road, next to the Arcade Cinema. This office was the third to be used for this purpose in Camberley. The first in the 1870s was on the corner of the High Street and the London Road, opposite the Cambridge Hotel. The second was a small shop just to the left of this building. This third office, which opened in 1892, was built by Dungay & Sons, the Princess Street builders. In 1937 James Page purchased these premises to extend his department store and create a double frontage with a second entrance on the London Road.

Charles and Mary Cleeve had used this small bungalow with its shop front in Princess Street as a greengrocer's until it was sold to Percy Holloway. Percy, who was born in Wiltshire in 1881, came to Camberley in 1901 and worked for Phillips Bros, a cycle firm with a branch in the High Street. Phillips's closed down in 1927 and Percy opened his shop in the same year. Cycling was his great love and he was instrumental in founding the Camberley Wheelers' Club before the Second World War. As chairman and member he rode in many of its races and competitions. Percy retired from the business in 1961 and his son Cyril took over until the premises were demolished in the redevelopment of the town in the 1970s. He died on his 86th birthday, 7 May 1967. This is now the site of the main post office.

Part of the Osnaburgh Parade, just opposite St Michael's Church, the London Road, in the mid-1930s. In 1932 the shops, from left to right, were H. Cottrell, hairdresser; A. Eighteen, fishmonger; and A. Gayler, fruiterer. By 1938 Mr Cottrell had changed his trade to selling antiques, Mr Eighteen had sold out to P. Kelliher and the empty shop became T. Jackson, greengrocer. All of these tradesmen lived above their shops.

Below: Following down Osnaburgh Parade were the shops on either side of the lane, which led to Plantation Row. The entrance to the lane was lined with two small dwellings known as Arch Cottages. George Dance, who is pictured at the upper window, owned the jeweller's shop. It is more commonly remembered as Hayes the jewellers, as it was purchased by Clement Hayes in 1936. The display of goods sold here looks rather sparse, especially when compared with the mouth-watering array of sweets in Mrs Day's confectionery shop.

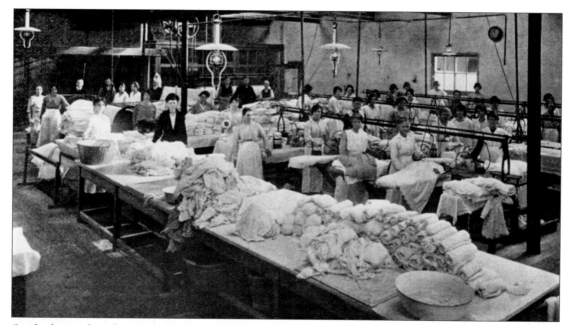

Camberley and Yorktown Laundry Company was founded in 1898 in Cromwell Road, just off King's Ride. The laundry was set up at this time because of the rapid growth of Camberley and Yorktown, both commercially and residentially, and also because of the influence of the army in the area at the Military College. Army officers' wives employed staff to do most of their household chores, but after the First World War it was difficult to recruit domestic staff and sending the laundry to a reliable company was a very good alternative. Many people had busy lives with little time to do their own laundry. A doorstep collection and delivery service by horse and cart was provided in the early days and this was replaced in the 1920s by a small van. In the late 1920s the directors were Alderman Sparvell, Mr F. Baker of Sadler & Baker Estate Agents, Dr A.T. Wooldridge and Mr W.W. Collins of Barclays Bank. In 1946, after the laundry changed its name to Household Cleaning Services, it was one of the first local companies to offer a dry cleaning service. In 1950, when Hale Laundry Ltd purchased the Camberley business, the services it offered were expanded to include home spring cleaning; curtains, carpets and furnishings would be taken to the cleaner's, while floors would be polished, windows washed, chimneys swept and paint and varnish cleaned and brightened.

New gas and electricity showrooms, Yorktown. The Yorktown & District Gas and Electricity Co. was formed at a general meeting with the inhabitants of Yorktown and Blackwater at the Duke of York Hotel on 16 December 1858, to consider the possibility of lighting the towns with gas. The company was registered in February 1859 and in December 1862 the work to erect the facilities had been completed. The entrance to the site was just east of the Blackwater Bridge and south of the London Road. Gas was supplied to a very limited area during the next twenty years, but after 1890 the supply was extended to Frimley, Hawley and Yateley. Over the following forty-six years gas output increased from 5 million cu. ft to 310 million cu. ft per year, fired by coal which arrived by rail to a siding off the main line. The electricity supply commenced in Camberley in December 1921. The new showrooms, offices and a further gasholder at Yorktown were opened on 8 December 1937 by MP Geoffrey Nicholson.

Members of the White family and staff. Percy White, who founded the company of White's in Camberley, was born in Wadhurst, Sussex, in 1875. He moved to Camberley in 1906 and opened his first business two years later selling motor-cycles, bicycles, gramophones and sewing machines from a shop close to where the Arena Leisure Centre is today. He installed the first petrol pump in the town and sold his first Morris car in 1919. He purchased a Dennis charabanc in August 1920 and in 1921 he initiated the first bus service from Camberley to London. In 1924 a trip every Wednesday from the town to Wembley cost 6s return. He puchased the garage site between the Cambridge Hotel and Knoll Road for £700 and built a temporary garage on this field (which had previously been used for growing cabbages) until he could make enough money for a more permanent building. Percy retired in 1955 and his son Richard took over the business.

A charabanc trip, ready to leave, outside the Camberley Working Men's Club, Obelisk Street.

Inside the office of White's of Camberley, photographed by Marshall & Son, in the 1930s. This group of ladies includes Helen Terry, Pamela Peters, Betty Price, M. Davies and some identified only by their Christian names of Sheila, Betty, Joan, Connie and Dona.

The staff dinner for employees of White's of Camberley was held at the Agincourt Hall on Monday 17 April 1939. During this period a celebration was held in April for those who worked for Percy White as this was the month in which he opened his first business. In common with most working-class dinners of the time, it was bottles of beer that accompanied the meal rather than the wine we expect today.

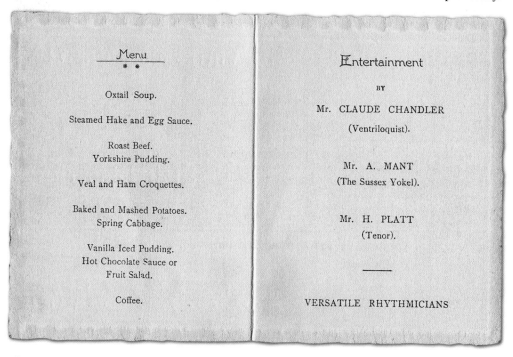

Menu
**

Oxtail Soup.

Steamed Hake and Egg Sauce.

Roast Beef.
Yorkshire Pudding.

Veal and Ham Croquettes.

Baked and Mashed Potatoes.
Spring Cabbage.

Vanilla Iced Pudding.
Hot Chocolate Sauce or
Fruit Salad.

Coffee.

Entertainment

BY

Mr. CLAUDE CHANDLER
(Ventriloquist).

Mr. A. MANT
(The Sussex Yokel).

Mr. H. PLATT
(Tenor).

———

VERSATILE RHYTHMICIANS

The menu and entertainment for White's employees, 1939.

6

Leisure & Sport

The Regal Cinema, Osnaburgh Parade, the London Road.

The Regal Cinema, Osnaburgh Parade, the London Road, opening night, August 1932. The ceremony was performed by Alan Butterworth JP, Chairman of the Frimley & Camberley Urban District Council, in front of twelve hundred people, with hundreds turned away. The cinema was completed in six months and concentrated on showing mainly British films. The interior of the cinema had been fitted out in an artistic and luxurious manner without being ultra-modern. The lighting from the ceiling and wall pillars was unusually effective, and with a large screen and state-of-the-art projection apparatus, ensured a perfect view from the back of the long auditorium. The first part of the opening programme was a news film, followed by Laurel and Hardy in *One Good Turn*. Then, after a musical interlude by The County Syncopaters, came the main attraction: Jack Hulbert and Cicely Courtneidge in *Jack's the Boy*. After the programme an informal reception was held in the Regal Café; Mrs May, wife of the chairman of Regal Ltd, cut a cake in honour of the occasion and thanked Mr Butterworth for opening the cinema. Later the venue was known as the Odeon and for the last few years as Robin's.

Clearing the site for Camberley swimming pool, February 1934.

In 1934 the demand for an outdoor swimming pool in Camberley was met with the sale of a plot of land belonging to Dr Atkinson of Portesbury House. This land was purchased by the Blue Pool (Camberley) Co. Ltd, who then contracted Musselwhites to build the pool. The site for the pool was ideally situated in a hollow which dipped steeply away from the London Road, about 300yds from the end of the High Street, with the wooded Portesbury Hill rising up behind it. The site was cleared on 22 February 1934 and by 7 March the outline of the pool was evident and the foundations for the tea house were in place. Building continued at a rapid pace and the pool was completed and opened on Thursday 24 May to a private view and on Saturday 26 May, to the public. The pool was 120ft long, 50ft wide and sloped from 3½ to 8ft; it was designed to accommodate 500 people, with 75 changing cubicles, catering facilities and parking for 60 cars. After nearly forty years, the local council acquired the pool in 1973, but it closed during 1976 because of the substantial cost of renovation. The pool did not reopen in 1977 and the site was eventually sold to developers in 1982.

Digging the foundations, March 1934.

The completed swimming pool, May 1934.

Marquees on the London Road Recreation Ground. Frimley & Camberley UDC purchased the land for the recreation ground in 1898 for £2,000 and the park subsequently laid out was named the London Road Recreation Ground. Shown here is a typical event held throughout the 100 years of the recreation ground's existence. The band plays, the marquees are set up and the sun is shining at one of the inter-war events. The houses to the rear of the marquee are those in Grand Avenue. The British Legion held their sports meetings here between the wars; these were well coordinated events under the chairmanship of Mr E.D. Brewer. Some of the events were tug-of-war, a baby show, fancy dress and a beauty show with a first prize of £5 5s. There were also a guess the weight of the cake competition and a pillow fight! A full athletics programme for children and adults was conducted under the Amateur Athletics Association rules; there were cash prizes for the first three past the tape. In 1922 the music was provided by the Sandhurst Prize Band. Currently the open space does not front the London Road as the Arena Leisure Centre has been built on this area of former parkland.

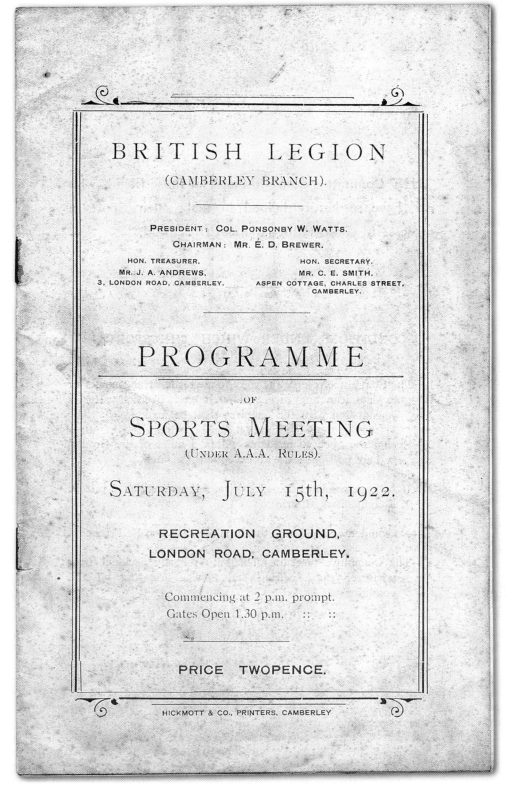

BRITISH LEGION
(CAMBERLEY BRANCH).

PRESIDENT : COL. PONSONBY W. WATTS.
CHAIRMAN : MR. E. D. BREWER.

HON. TREASURER.
MR. J. A. ANDREWS,
3, LONDON ROAD, CAMBERLEY.

HON. SECRETARY.
MR. C. E. SMITH,
ASPEN COTTAGE, CHARLES STREET,
CAMBERLEY.

PROGRAMME

OF

SPORTS MEETING
(UNDER A.A.A. RULES).

SATURDAY, JULY 15th, 1922.

**RECREATION GROUND,
LONDON ROAD, CAMBERLEY.**

Commencing at 2 p.m. prompt.
Gates Open 1.30 p.m.   ::   ::

PRICE TWOPENCE.

HICKMOTT & CO., PRINTERS, CAMBERLEY

A British Legion Programme of a Sports Meeting, 15 June 1922.

The foundation stone for the pavilion in the London Road Recreation Ground was laid in June 1898. It was designed by W.J. Hodgson and built at a cost of £275 by Martin Wells & Co. The total cost of erecting it was paid for by local businessmen and residents, who included HRH the Crown Prince of Siam, who lived in Camberley at that time. When pictured here in the 1930s it was used primarily as changing rooms for sports teams and the committee which organised the Camberley Carnival also met here.

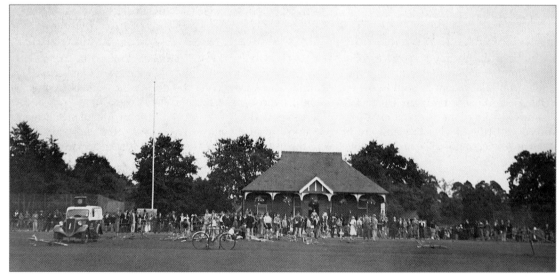

Camberley Wheelers' Cycle Club, London Road Recreation Ground. Camberley Wheelers was the local cycling club that organised road races and events in and around the town. Here, a large group of cyclists and their supporters were photographed in the 1930s, with the sound-system van and its loudspeaker on the roof ready to announce the results. Mr Holloway, who had a cycle shop in Princess Street, was one of the founding members of this club.

A combined emergency services exercise, held at the London Road Recreation Ground in the 1930s. The St John Ambulance Brigade and the British Red Cross Society both had branches in Camberley. The St John Ambulance can be seen in the background. This local section was part of the Guildford Corps, of which Field-Marshal HRH the Duke of Connaught (who lived at Bagshot Park) was Grand Prior of the Venerable Order of the Hospital of St John of Jerusalem. The Red Cross and St John Ambulance Brigade worked with the local police and fire brigade at all local functions and provided first-aid posts, road accident services and sick comfort depots before the introduction of the National Health Service.

A view looking across part of the football pitch in the London Road Recreation Ground towards the London Road, in the early 1930s. Just behind the goalposts are the newly erected public conveniences that were built in August 1930. These were some of the first facilities along the main A30 road after leaving London and they became a regular stop-off point for motor travellers. The cottage to the right used to stand in the grounds of the Staff College opposite St Tarcisius's Church. The cottage was demolished in the 1960s.

The new tennis courts and surrounding gardens, London Road Recreation Ground, on the day they opened to the public in 1925, with the metal railings that were laid along the boundary with Southwell Park Road.

The first game of bowls to be played on the new green at London Road Recreation Ground, in May 1925, with Frank Stallwood on the far right and David Sparvell in front of him about to play the first wood. The first bowling club in Camberley was formed in June 1906. Originally known as the Victoria Bowling Club, members played on a green just behind the Victoria Hotel. These two new greens were laid out at a cost of £89, which included fencing the site.

Action on the bowling green, London Road Recreation Ground, Camberley.

Camberley Carnival. 'The Costers' Day Out', posing in Upper Charles Street.

Hospital funding today is primarily provided by the government under the National Health Service, which was formed in 1947. Before this, funds were raised at a local level by donations and special events, such as an annual carnival. The Camberley Carnival was a huge event, which took place in July each year, the proceeds going to the Frimley and Camberley District Hospital. The carnival organising committee was formed with approximately 150 members, chaired by Captain T. Loman. Preparations for the Camberley Carnival started in March or April each year with the carnival usually taking place in mid-July. Many events took place during carnival week at the London Road Recreation Ground and in local halls, such as a darts tournament, treasure hunt, push-ball matches, motor-cycle trick racing and firework displays. Other features for the week included a whist drive, motor treasure hunt, swimming gala (at the Blue Pool, Camberley) and a Grand Gala Radio Star Variety Performance at the Regal Cinema. Camberley Bowling Club arranged a friendly bowling match against a Surrey County select team. The carnival procession generally took two hours to tour the town, starting at College Town gates and finishing in The Avenue. Up to 20,000 people lined the streets to watch the array of floats and awards were made for the most imaginative ones.

Camberley Carnival, 'Coronation Quads'.

The Camberley Carnival Queen, Ann Lowe (centre) and her attendants pose just before her Coronation by Admiral Sir Frederick Tudor, July 1939. From the left, the girls are Pamela Dismore (18) of King's Ride, Julie Digance (25) of Uplands Road and Eileen Stanley, the Deputy Queen, (16), of Victoria Road. The Queen, Ann Lowe, of Moorlands Road, was brought up in Canada and had only moved to Camberley in 1937. Aged 19, she was attended by her page, Miss Joy Lawrence, the eight-year-old daughter of the organiser of the event. Next to Joy is Edna Trowbridge (18), a nursemaid who lived in The Avenue, then Gladys Warner of Station Road, Frimley. The lady on the right is Mrs Joan Sanker aged (22), of Brook Road. The attendants' dresses were white with crimson spots and the Queen's cape and the page's jacket were both crimson.

The Camberley Heath Golf Club buildings were designed by the local architects, H.R. and B.A. Poulter. The Golf Club was formed in June 1912 and plans for the clubhouse were submitted in November of that year. The building was erected by George Kemp & Sons at a cost of £3,987. The men who formed this club were Mr J.F. Wright of Frimley Hall, Herbert John Butler Hollings of Watchetts, Vice-Admiral Johnstone of Graitney, Mr Temple Cooke of Edmonscote and local solicitor Edmond Close. In the 1930s the patron of the club was the Duke of Connaught. The annual subscription for men was 8 guineas and for lady members 5 guineas; this also entitled them to use the tennis and croquet courts on site.

A programme for Crawley Hill Women's Institute's production of *Pearl the Fishermaiden*, 1934. The opening meeting of the Crawley Hill branch of the Women's Institute was held in the Maple Leaf Hut (later Caird Hall), Crawley Hill, at 3 p.m. on 12 October 1922. The meeting was opened by the President, who, in a few well-chosen words, hoped the hut would provide as much pleasure for the WI as it did for the Cadet Corps who kindly lent the hut to the institute. After the speeches an excellent tea and musical entertainment was provided. Musical entertainment appeared to be a particular forte of the Crawley Hill WI, which presented operettas annually at Caird Hall. In 1934 two performances of *Pearl the Fishermaiden* were performed on 1 February at 3 p.m. and 7.45 p.m. The part of Pearl was played by Veronica Maxwell and the leading 'man', Lorenzo, by Miss C. Manby. The dancing was ably presented by the Mortimer School of Dancing (later to become Elmhurst Ballet School).

CRAWLEY HILL WOMEN'S INSTITUTE.

An OPERETTA

ENTITLED

PEARL THE FISHERMAIDEN

(Under the direction of Mrs. RIGG)

at

CAIRD HALL

on

THURSDAY, FEBRUARY 1st, 1934.

MATINEE - AT 3 P.M.

EVENING PERFORMANCE AT 7.45 P.M.

PROGRAMME

The cast of *Pearl the Fishermaiden*, February 1934.

The annual Cadet Corps' Fête at Collingwood Grange was a notable event in the social calendar for the residents of Frimley and Camberley. The Frimley and Camberley Cadet Corps was founded in 1908 as a direct result of an earlier Bible Class set up by Grace Reynolds. In 1903 she had been in charge of boys between 15 and 18 years of age who attended services at St Paul's Church. In 1904 she visited Canada and brought back a maple leaf tie-pin for each boy, which they decided to use as a badge. Inspired by Lord Robert's National Service League, and with the help of her father who gave £100 towards the purchase of uniforms and Mr Hoare, an ex-corporal in the Coldstream Guards, she established the first meeting of this military group which still flourishes today. In 1912 the Cadet Corps was affilated to the territorial force and had the subsequent honour of being attached to the 5th Battalion of the Queen's Royal West Surrey Regiment. Here HRH the Duchess of Gloucester, who opened the fête in 1936, is talking to General Sir William Furse and Brigadier-General Jelf.

At each annual Cadet Corps' Fête local people were encouraged to spend as much as they could afford, and various stalls were set out around the gardens in an attempt to attract income. The small 'swiss-cottage' in the background was probably used by a local fortune-teller. The gentleman talking to the lady in costume was Comptroller of the Household of the Duke of Connaught at Bagshot Park, Captain Fitzroy Fyers.

The mock gypsy encampment at the Cadet Corps' Fête, Collingwood Grange, 1936.

Another royal visitor to the fête in 1936, was Princess Marie Louise, seen here with Brigadier-General Jelf.

Mr W.A. James, Headmaster of Camberley School, with a group of boys who were setting about 'Digging for Victory' in the autumn of 1939. Children were actively encouraged to join in this campaign and the owners of the large local houses gave over plots to be used. This group with their spades ready for use is probably in the grounds of Portesbury House or France Hill House.

7

Religion & Education

St Michael's Church in Yorktown was designed by Henry Woodyer and built of local sarsen stone in the Victorian Gothic style. The church was consecrated by Dr Sumner, Bishop of Winchester, in January 1851. Originally the church consisted of a nave, chancel and a small bell tower, which was removed in the mid-twentieth century. The spire, designed by Arnold Hoole and built by Norris & Sons of Sunningdale, was erected in 1891. A plaque in the belfry reads: 'The tower and spire of this Church were built by Ellen Middleton and her husband Frederick Matthews Middleton – to the Glory of God and the dear memory of their beloved daughter, Freda. AD 1891'.

The chancel of St Michael's Church in Yorktown, with the beautifully carved reredos, was designed and made by Professor Edward de la Motte, who was attached to the Royal Military College. It was erected in 1883 in memory of a former student at the Staff College, Lieutenant Porter, who lost his life through an accident on HMS *Oxenholme* when on his way to join the expeditionary force in Egypt. Henry Gomm, the landlord of the Crown public house at Yorktown, created the round stone corbels, which are set all around the walls of the nave depicting scenes from the Bible, surrounded by carved sprays of leaves and flowers. The work took him over six years to complete.

Opposite: The graveyard surrounding St Michael's Church in Yorktown is a reminder of the close association the church had with military personnel as well as the civilian population. There are at least two men buried here who were awarded a Victoria Cross, Sergeant-Major William Lendrim and Thomas A. Butler. A young boy living in Camberley described watching one of their funerals in 1891. He went 'down to the College to see a grand Military funeral. The man whose name was Major Lendrim had won the Victoria Cross for bravery at the Crimean War. Every one of the RMC cadets, freemasons of Blackwater, Royal Engineers, the regiment of which he belonged, all the college servants, officers, professors and friends of the deceased were there, in number about 2,000. It started from the Staff College and the college band played (muffled drums) Dead March in Saul and The Girl I Left Behind Me alternatively whilst the coffin on a cannon covered with the most lovely wreaths was conducted to the College church . . . the Revd headed the procession to the cemetery where the coffin was lowered and three volleys (twenty-four guns) were fired.'

The treble bell from St Michael's Church, Yorktown. The treble bell, with a diameter of 29in and weighing over 6cwt, was erected in memory of Ellen and Freda Middleton, the wife and daughter of the Vicar of St Michael's Church, the Revd F.M. Middleton. St George's Church in Camberley was built in memory of his wife Ellen, who died in 1892, and the spire of St Michael's Church, in which these bells hang, was built in memory of his daughter Freda. The largest bell, which is 40in diameter, was presented by the parishioners as a mark of respect for the twenty-seven years Mr Middleton spent at this parish. In January 1936 the bells in the spire of St Michael's Church had to be taken down and sent to John Taylor & Sons' foundry. These eight bells were hung in 1895 and had originally been placed in an oak frame, built with 12in timbers. Although the timbers were sound there had been some movement in the frame and it was decided that they should renew the fastening mechanism and install them in an iron frame. All the bells were made in the key of F major and were cast by John Warner & Sons at Cripplegate in London.

The old Congregational church in Obelisk Street, Camberley, just before it was demolished in 1930. This church was built before 1879 as a mission room or out-station to serve the people in this rapidly growing area of Camberley, and to save them the walk to St Michael's Church in Yorktown. The new St George's Church in Knoll Road was built in 1892, replacing this chapel for Church of England parishioners; the small chapel became known as the Obelisk Street Free Church. In 1909 thirty-two members of the Yorktown Baptist Church formed a breakaway group who worshipped here and these worshippers had, by 1915, become part of the congregational faith.

Two views of the interior of the Congregational church Camberley. At this time the minister was the Revd H.C. Pugh MA who arrived in Camberley on 22 October 1924 and lived at Girvan in Park Road. He was instrumental in the drive to raise money for a new church, which was built in 1930 on the corner of Southwell Park Road and Southern Road. The traditional gifts for Harvest Festival, including the bread made to resemble a sheaf of wheat, are lined up in front of the pulpit, which it is believed was formerly used by Charles Kingsley when he was the minister at Eversley church.

The Catholic iron church (dedicated to St Tarcisius) and Presbytery in the early 1920s. On 19 August 1869, in Mr Critchfield's Staff Hotel, the London Road, and in the house of John Hughes at 5 London Road, mass was first celebrated and continued in both places until 1874. Thanks to the generosity of Lady Southwell, a building which served as a school during the week and a church on Sunday was erected in Obelisk Street in November 1874. Father J.B. McKenna was appointed the first priest of the Camberley Mission, and his successor, Father O'Neill, collected sufficient funds to build the iron church, which opened in 1884. By 1920 this church was in a poor state of repair.

Father Patrick Twomey in the grounds of St Tarcisius's Church, Camberley, with the houses, which stood in Charles Street and Upper Charles Street behind him. Father Twomey was parish priest from 1906 until 1950. Born in Macroom, County Cork, in 1876, he entered St Patrick's College, Maynooth, where he was ordained in June 1901. He enjoyed riding his horse around the parish and joining the local hunt. He raised money for the building of the church by holding a horse show in Camberley. He loved greyhounds, one of whom can be seen with him.

Opposite, bottom: The new St Tarcisius's Church, Camberley. Funds had been collected for a new church since 1908 and £2,600 was banked by 1914. The building of the new church was postponed owing to increased building costs and the First World War. Building commenced on 1 July 1923, the foundation stone being laid on 12 September by the Bishop of Southwark. The church was designed by Mr F.A. Walters. Further subscriptions and funds from other sources increased the total collected to £9,000, the final cost being £12,500. The church was opened on 18 November 1924 and consecrated on 26 June 1926 by the Right Revd W.F. Brown, Bishop of Pella. The church is a memorial to the Catholic officers who attended the RMA and Staff College and lost their lives during the First World War. Their names are inscribed on panels inside the church.

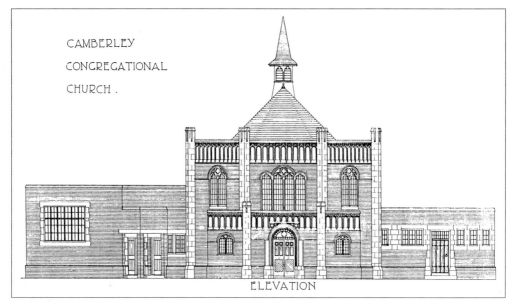

Plan for the Congregational church. The land on which the Congregational church was erected was purchased by two local businessmen, fishmonger and poulterer Nicholas Verran, who also gave the land on which St Mary's Church was built, and James Page, who owned the department store in the High Street. It was designed by Maurice Lawson, James Page's brother-in-law, who was an architect in the town. The church was built at a cost of £5,500.

The opening ceremony of the Congregational church in Southwell Park Road, 23 October 1930. The men who had worked for years on this project are watched by a crowd of onlookers that attended the ceremony to celebrate the completion of the church. It was formally opened by Alec E. Glassy MP, with the Revd J.O. Jones of Bournemouth offering the Prayer of Dedication. On the extreme right of the group is William Wells King, who built the church with two former ministers of the old church in Obelisk Street, Messrs Pugh and Kent-Smith, next to him. The minister in charge in 1930, the Revd A.W. Austin, is second from the left.

The entrance to Camberley Congregational church in Southwell Park Road, illuminated to enhance what was described as its domestic Gothic style. The large upper windows had slightly tinted glass to throw a warm light into the body of the church, producing a bright and singularly cheerful effect.

The laying of the foundation stone at St Mary's Church in Park Road, Camberley, 30 June 1937. Bishop Golding Bird of Guildford is on the left and the Revd Mr Partridge, Vicar of St Peter's at Frimley, right of centre. After the ceremony 100 people had afternoon tea at the old corrugated-iron church in the Frimley Road. St Mary's was designed by Mr G.G. Lofting, built by the local Camberley firm of William Wells King and was dedicated by the Bishop of Guildford on 22 December 1937.

The Royal Albert Orphanage in the 1930s.

The Royal Albert Orphanage was situated among the Surrey pines on the Chobham Ridges, south of the Portsmouth Road and west of the Maultway. The drive to the orphanage was located a few hundred yards from the Jolly Farmer roundabout on the Portsmouth Road. The orphanage was founded in 1864 and opened on 29 December in the same year, as a memorial to the Prince Consort. Fifty boys and fifty-two girls lived there; however, girls were not accepted after March 1903. After this period the orphanage had accommodation for 140 boys, the age of admission was between 5 and 13, and the leaving age was 16. Most of the boys were admitted to the orphanage having been selected from a list of candidates in May and November; no fee was required. Financial support for the orphanage was dependent on donations, subscriptions and collection boxes. Some donors were entitled to certain privileges, for example a donation of £250 entitled the donor during his lifetime to have one boy always looked after at the orphanage. The boys were educated and trained in a manner which would enable them to obtain employment. Approximately 100 boys attended lessons and the remaining forty were engaged on various trades or on the farm. Training was available to them as gardeners, farmers, carpenters, tailors, printers, shoe-repairers, bakers or office workers, depending on their suitability. The physical well-being of the boys was also looked after, particularly during the summer holidays, when those who had no home to go to could enjoy the open-air life at the annual camp. They were often visited by royalty; the Duke of Gloucester, Lady Patricia Ramsay, Lady Beatrice Meade and the President, HRH the Duke of Connaught, who came on Commemoration Day to present prizes. The orphanage became the Royal Albert School from 20 February 1942 and closed in January 1954, when the children were moved to Gatton Park near Reigate. The orphanage building was destroyed by fire in 1987 and the area is now part of the Wellington Park Housing Estate.

Tailors workshop, Royal Albert Orphanage.

The Royal Albert Orphanage recreation area.

An exterior view of Yorktown School, the London Road, in the 1930s with the original school building on the left, which opened in 1871, and the newer infant school on the right, which was erected in 1906. The original building was designed by Charles Buckeridge of London without the distinctive bell-tower which is such a focal point today. In 1932 the headmaster was Mr R.S. Allen, the headmistress Miss A.L. Jackson and the head of the infant school was Mrs M.R. Cartwright.

Opposite, top: The main classroom at Yorktown School, in the 1930s. In this photograph the shutters are drawn back: they were used to divide the room into two separate units. When the school was erected there were just three classrooms: the infant room, which was on the west side of the building; the main room for teaching all children from the infant stage until they left school and went to work; and a very small classroom behind it overlooking the girls yard or playground. Initially the children would have sat in raised or tiered seating with the masters calling down small groups to work with him at the board or at his desk. A pupil teacher, invariably an older pupil, would have taught other groups in the same room. In the 1930s the infant classes were taught in the adjoining building and this room was used for school assembly or for educating two classes of children.

Opposite, bottom: Classroom, Yorktown School, Camberley. This type of wooden partitioning with a glazed upper half was used in most of the local schools including Camberley and Frimley. It enabled borrowed light to filter into classrooms like this small one at Yorktown School, which was situated at the rear of the building facing north.

The Knoll, Camberley, a school for young ladies.

The new Frimley and Camberley Grammar School, just after it opened on 9 December 1931. Children who had won a grammar school place before the opening of the school had to travel to Woking, Farnham or Egham. Asked to recall what it was like to arrive there in 1931, pupils said it was 'enormous, grand, magnificent, with hundreds of doors and passages' and one girl thought it would 'hold all Camberley'. The school moved to new buildings on the Old Dean Estate in 1967 and these premises were used as an annexe to France Hill School until 1971. They currently house the Watchetts School.

Opposite: Ladies doubles, The Knoll, Camberley. The Knoll was built in the 1860s for Revd Sir George William Cox; this was the first house built in Knoll Road and was named after the knoll on which the Obelisk stands. Sir George Cox, together with Mr Atkinson of Portesbury House and Mr Sparvell, the local baker and first Alderman of Frimley & Camberley UDC, were jointly responsible for changing the name of Cambridge Town to Camberley. At the time these photographs were taken, in the early 1920s, The Knoll was a girl's school. The house was owned by the Revd A.C. Fox, who let the building to Miss Wilding in 1913 on a twenty-one year lease at an annual rent of £300 for use as a school for young ladies. The Knoll was used as a school until 1939 and was then requisitioned by the Army during the war as a de-briefing centre for the Royal Engineers. After the war The Knoll was used for temporary housing by the council and divided into family units by 1946. In 1956 the house and grounds, including the Obelisk, were purchased by Father W. Quinlan, parish priest at St Tarcisius's Church, for use as a school for Roman Catholic children. It was intended that the original house be used as a hall for assembly and other functions. A new school for 350 pupils was built in the grounds at a proposed cost of £40,000. All the buildings were demolished for housing in 1996.

BIBLIOGRAPHY

Mitchell, P., Townsend, S. and Shelmerdine, M., *The Surrey Border and Camberley Railway*, Brighton, Plateway Press, 1993

Mockford-Ferryman, A.F. Major, *Annals of Sandhurst*, London, William Heinemann, 1900

Potten, I., *Looking back in Longing*, Ilfracombe, Arthur H. Stockwell Ltd, 1985